The Secret City of the Great King!

(HOW the True Church will Escape from the Great Tribulation!)

By
The Worldwide People's Revolution!®

Book 042 ♥

(A Photo of a Ferris Wheel — P-5877)

Copyright, Dedication and Introduction

By our Selected King's Chief Editor,
Doctor Samuel Walker Edison, Ph.D., MA, BS and QC!

ISBN — 13:978-1727-5964-10
ISBN — 10:1727-5964-12

00-01 [_] This Inspired Book is COPYRIGHTED AD 2018—4020, by **The Worldwide People's Revolution!®**, whose Selected King is the Man with the Spirit of Elijah, who is the Inspired Author of more than 350 Good Books, among which you can Discover the New MAGNIFIED Version of the entire *Holy Bible, The Book of Mormon, the Koran,* and a Multitude of Spiritual Books, as well as Unique Books that address various Important Subjects — such as: **"The New RIGHTEOUS One-World Government!" (HOW to Establish a Righteous One-World Government without Going to WAR!) By The Worldwide People's Revolution!®** Book 056.

00-02 [_] All Rights are Reserved for the Truth's Sake. No Portion of this Amazing Book shall be Reproduced by any Means for Sale without Written Permission from **The Worldwide People's Revolution!®**, which is Determined to do its Best to Help Bring Down the Evil Empire, whereby this MADNESS can come to an END! However, with our Permission, anyone in the World may Reproduce Exact Copies of this Unique Book, and Sell it for a Reasonable Price, and KEEP 90 percent of the Net Profits for themselves: because our Selected King only Wants 10% of the Net Profits for the Construction of **"The Great World TEMPLE of PEACE,"** in Jerusalem, which will the Tallest and Largest Building in the World, which will be the Headquarters for **"The New RIGHTEOUS One-World Government!"** {See www.Amazon.com for: **"The CONSTITUTION for the New RIGHTEOUS One-World GovernMINT!" (How all Peoples can get True Justice, and Celebrate the Great Year of JUBILEE!)**, Book 016, plus: **"The Great World TEMPLE of PEACE!" (The Glory of Jerusalem Arises Again!) By The Worldwide People's Revolution!®** Book 017.}

00-03 [_] This Inspired Book is now DEDICATED to all of those Wise People, who Accept what Jesus Christ stated in *Luke 21:36: "Watch you therefore, and always Pray to God: so that you may be Accounted Worthy to Escape all of those Evil Things that shall come to pass, and to Stand in front of the Son of the Man of Holiness with a Clean Conscience."* — The New MAGNIFIED Version (NMV)

00-04 [_] O Doctor Edison, that is NOT how my *King James Version* reads; and therefore, I do not Believe it. Indeed, if it is not written in my *Bible,* I do not Believe it.

00-05 [_] Well, I suppose that you would also not Believe that Men Landed on the Moon, just because it is not written in your *Unholy Mutilated Bible,* huh?

00-06 [_] NO, I do NOT Believe that Men Landed on the Moon, nor that your Selected King is the Man with the Spirit of Elijah: beCause that is the single most Ridiculous Thing that I have ever Heard! Indeed, God would not Use an Ignorant FOOL like him to Write his Inspired Words of Provable Truths: beCause that would Confound us Worldly-wise People, whereby we might make Fools of ourselves, which would be Em-bare-assing to us Professing "Christians," who are going to be RAPTURED up to Heaven before the Great Tribulation. †§‡§§

(HOW the True Church will Escape from the Great Tribulation!)

00-07 [_] O Doctor Samuel Walker Edison, what are the Symbols (†§‡§§) for? Moreover, is that Picture of the most Flowery Church in the Whole World some of your doings?

00-08 [_] Well, our Selected King uses those Symbols for Wise Purposes, which are Explained in Details within his first 30 Inspired Books, if you Want to Learn what they Mean. Indeed, there is no Need for Wasting any Space within this Book to Repeat all such Things, much less to Cause any Boredom to Faithful Readers, who Want NEW Information. Therefore, you will just have to "Reed" one of those Books, or at least a Book Preview on www.Amazon.com. And as for that Flowery Church, just try to Imagine how Distasteful the Picture would be in Black and White, without any Multitude of Cheerful Colors, as it has in Reality? Indeed, the *King James Version of the Holy Bible* is Colorless, when Compared with the New MAGNIFIED Version of it. But, if you Doubt it, just Study the Book Previews that are Free of all Charges on Amazon. Go to Google, and Search for **The Worldwide People's Revolution!®**, and then Amaze yourself with what you can Discover. It is one Fantastic Collection of Pure Inspiration! Be Sure to Carefully Read ALL of the Book Descriptions before you Read the Book Previews. I Suggest that you begin with the Book Description for: **"Guaranteed Solutions!" (HOW to Solve our Local and Global Problems in the Most Rational Manner Possible!) By The Worldwide People's Revolution!®** Book 080.

00-09 [_] O Doctor Sam, WHY do you "spel sum uv yoor Werdz in Swanky Funetik Ingglish"? Do you Sincerely Believe that most Professing "Christians" will be Able to Understand all such "KUNFUUZHUN"? †§

00-10 [_] Well, my Friend, in normal English Confusion, there are more than 300 Different Ways to Spell only 30 Simple English Sounds, which is also Thoroughly Explained in some of our Selected King's first 30 Books, which you can find on www.Amazon.com / usa for your Great Enlightenment and True Education. {See: **"The Public School of IGNERUNT FQLZ!" (How we have been GRAATLEE DISEEVD by Capitalism!)**, Book 024, plus: **"Are you a Jobless Graduate of the SKQL uv FQLZ?" (HOW to get a GOUD EJUKAASHUN without Robbing the Bank!)**, Book 020, plus: **"In thu Beeginingz uv Thingz!" (Thu Kreeaashun Stooree frum thu Beegining!) By The Worldwide People's Revolution!®** Book 025.}

00-11 [_] O Doctor Sam, WHY are so many of your Words CAPITALIZED? Is that Proper English? Will you and your Selected King not get into Trouble with God during the Day of Judgment, just for Capitalizing Faith, Hope, Trust, Love, Patience, Persistence, and OBEDIENCE, which are **"The Seven Basic Spiritual Building Blocks of LIFE!"** — which are also the Seven Basic Building Blocks of DEATH, if we Believe LIES, and set our Hope on MEN, instead of GOD, and Trust in Buzzeldick the Great to SAVE us for Positions within the Holy Kingdom of the GODS, while Loving the EVIL Works of the Synagogue of SATAN, who Inspired Evil Men to Invent all Kinds of ABOMINATIONS — such as those Stinking Noisy Polluting CARS, Vans, Pickups, Buses, Trucks, Tractors, Bulldozers, Airplanes, Lawnmowers, Chainsaws, Weed-eaters, Snow Blowers, Snowmobiles, Garden Tillers, Motorcycles, Motor Scooters, Motorboats, and all of the EVILS that your Selected King has Listed in: **"The Nature of CAPITALISM!" (A List of the EVILS of CAPITALISM!)**, Book 038, which CONDEMNS our Wonderful Economic System to HELL, and leaves us Standing Stark Naked in front of the Judgment Bar of Almighty God, who said: *"Come you OUT from among the Wicked Ones, and be you SEPARATED from them, and Touch NONE of their UNCLEAN THINGS, says the Supreme Ruler your God; and then I will Receive you, and will be a Loving Father unto you, and you shall become my Adopted Sons* *and Purified Daughters, says the Almighty God!"* — See *Second Corinthians 6:17* and *Revelation 18:4,* in any Version you like, except for the *Gay King James Version*? †§‡§§

00-12 [_] Well, my Friend, I see that you are being very Sarcastic, which some Professing "Christians" would say is not very "Christ-like," even though it was very "Elijah-like," according to *First Kings 18:33.* Indeed, Elijah MOCKED the Baal Worshipers, even as you have Mocked them and their Abominations, which will have no Place in the Holy Kingdom of All that is GOOD.

00-13 [_] O Doctor Edison, HOW in the World could we get to WORK without our Cars? Are you saying that God has no Use for CARS? Will Jesus Christ Ride a DONKEY when he Establishes his New Righteous One-World Government over all of the Earth?

00-14 [_] Well, try not to Jump to any Irrational Conclusions, O Jackrabbit. Indeed, there is a Far Superior Way to Live, which our Selected King has Proven within many of his Good Books, which you have Obviously NOT "red," much less with a Capital R — with Faith, Hope, Trust, Love, Patience, Persistence, nor OBEDIENCE. Otherwise, you would now Know that we could all be Living in Manmade PARADISES! {See www.Amazon.com for: **"The Environmentalists' Paradise!" (HOW almost Everyone could be Living in a Beautiful Manmade Paradise!)**, Book 035, plus: **"UNLIMITED ENERJEE 99 Percent Pollutions Free!" (HOW to Obtain FREE ElecTrickery, Worldwide!)**, Book 029, plus: **"The Right Design for Living!" (A List of Great Advantages for Building Beautiful Planned City States!)**, Book 012, plus: **"A Sure Cure for GUN VIOLENCE!" (HOW TO STOP GANG WARS and CRIMINAL SHOOTINGS!)**, Book 031, plus: **"GLORIOUS Swanky Hotels Castles and Fortresses!" (Beautiful Planned City States for WISE Intelligent Well-Educated People with Common Sense and Good Understanding!)**, Book 019, plus: **"The Low Court of Supreme Injustices is Brought to Trial!" (Our Elected King Butts Heads with the United States Supreme Court, with or without their Black Robes of Hypocrisies and Lies!)**, Book 011, plus: **"AIIRMWVC and Reasonable Solutions!" (Aliens, Illegal Immigrants, Refugees, Migrant Workers and other Victims of Capitalism!)**, Book 032, plus: **"Poverty Hunger Riots Strikes Brutalities Election Deceptions and Civil Wars!" (The High Price that we Earthlings have Paid for Leaving the Good Land!)**, Book 014, plus: **"Does a Good Soldier have to be a MURDERER?" (Seven Great Swanky Armies of Voluntary Working Soldiers!)**, Book 027, plus: **"Mark Twain Races for the PRESIDENCY!" (The 2020 Presidential Candidates Desperately Need Some STRONG Undefeatable COMPETITION!)**, Book 033, plus: **"Thu Nq MAGNUFIID Verzhun uv Thu PROVERBZ uv KING SOLUMUN in Plaan Ingglish!" (The Understandable Version of the Famous Proverbs of King Solomon in Plain English!)** By The Worldwide People's Revolution!® Book 028, which is a Companion Book of: **"ECCLESIASTES UNCOVERED!" (The New MAGNIFIED Version of Ecclesiastes and the Song of Solomon in Plain English!)**, Book 034.

00-15 [_] O Doctor Edison, it would Require a HUNDRED THOUSAND YEARS to Read all such Books! Surely you do not Expect ME to "Reed" all of them, do you? §

00-16 [_] Well, if you Want to Escape from the Great Tribulation, you will have to: beCause you and everyone else has a LOT of Important Lessons to be Learned, which you cannot Learn from reading Childish Newspapers and Worthless Magazines.

The Fascinating Menu for a Feast of Provable Truths!

Chapter 01 — WHERE IS the Secret City of the Great King? ... 7

Chapter 02 — What does it MEAN to REPENT? ... 14

Chapter 03 — How many Different Kinds of Salvations are there?? ... 20

Chapter 04 — HOW to get the Nations Converted and SAVED! ... 24

Chapter 05 — A Good Heart, but a Bad Head! ... 27

Chapter 06 — How to Live in Peace in Spite of Terrorists! ... 29

Chapter 07 — The New MAGNIFIED Version of JAMES! ... 31

Chapter 08 — Please Forward to John McArdle ... 41

Chapter 09 — The Irreverent LOUDMOUTH Sloth-gut Windbag Hole-in-his-Head Delivers another LONG Boring Sarcastic Sermon! ... 43

Chapter 10 — Can the Eagle not be Hydrogen-powered? ... 49

Chapter 11 — WHO will Qualify to Escape? ... 51

Chapter 12 — Comforting Words for those People who are Left Behind ... 53

Chapter 13 — The Great Eagle will Land in Mount Zion ... 56

Chapter 14 — Will Alma and Abinadi be there when we get there? ... 58

Chapter 15 — Jesus Tells us what to Do, himself! ... 60

Chapter 16 — The Conclusion ... 62

The Enticement is on the Back Cover ... page 64

A Long List of other Fascinating Literature by the same Inspired Author ... 65

This Book contains about 40,000 Words and 3 Photographs, not counting the Cover Photo.

(HOW the True Church will Escape from the Great Tribulation!)

— Chapter 01 —

WHERE IS the Secret City of the Great King?

01-01 [_] *"Great is the Supreme Ruler, and Greatly to be Praised in the Holy City of our Savior God, even in the Mountains of his Holiness. Beautiful for Situation, the Joy of the Whole Earth, is Mount Zion, in the Recesses of the Uttermost Parts of the Far North, even the Holy City of the Great King! Yes, God is known in her Palaces for a Place of Refuge* — a Place to Run to and Hide during Times of Great Troubles. *Behold, the Kings of the Earth were once Assembled Together, and they Passed by it in Ships* — which Sailed from Tarshish, which is now called the Angel's Land: because the Angel Engla first Visited there, whereby it Obtained the Name of Englaland, which was later Changed to England — *yes, they saw it, and so they Marveled:* because it is a Great City with Tall Stone Walls, being more than 200 feet Tall, which Stand on the Top of High Cliffs on a large Plateau, which is Surrounded by 2 Raging Rivers in Deep Rocky Ravines, which no Man can Traverse, which Forms the Mighty Jordan River, which comes Out of the North, which Forms Huge Icebergs each Winter: because that River runs into a Deep Valley, which Freezes as the Sunstar Works its Way to the South, leaving the River in the Dark. Yes, the Water Builds Up and Backs Up for 400 Miles or more, while Filling the Jordan Valley, which Releases the Iceberg each Summer, when it Thaws Out enough to Allow the Water Pressure behind the Iceberg to Push it into the Artic Sea, where it Floats Away, which leaves the Jordan River Open for Ships to pass through it to Mount Zion, which has only one Entrance into the Holy City, which is Under the Waterfalls at the Foot of it, where the 2 Great Rivers Converge into One, which is the Mighty Jordan River, which is the Greatest River in the World, which comes Out of the Hollow Earth, which is the Paradise of God, which has its own Central Sun, which has much more Land than can be Found on the Outside of the Earth, where the Barbarians Live. Indeed, the Kings of the Earth were Gathered Together to go Visit Mount Zion; but, when they saw it *they were Greatly Troubled, and Hastened to get Away: beCause FEAR took hold upon them up there, and even Pains, as of a Woman who is in Travail* while giving Birth to a Baby: because the entire City was Glowing with the Glory of God, from which came forth Rainbow Colors like the Northern Lights, while Holy Angels Danced on the Top of the City Wall, being Giants 40 feet Tall, and having Wings a hundred feet Wide, being Dressed in White Robes with Bare Feets, who all Looked like one Holy Family, who were in Perfect Harmony, whose Skin Color was Danish Blond, having Great Blond Wings, Blue Eyes, and Rosy Cheeks, being in Perfect Health, having very Deep Muscular Chests; but, without Beards: because their Faces were Smooth, and their Blond Hairs were very Long and Beautiful and Flowing as they Danced Together with their Wings Folded Up, which was a Terrifying Sight to those Unholy Kings, who Fled the Scene in the Ships of Tarshish.

01-02 [_] *"You have Broken the Ships of Tarshish, O God, with an East Wind,* and left those Kings to Drown in the Sea, whereby only one Sailor Escaped on a Raft to tell the Sad and Happy Tale. Indeed, *as we have Heard, so have we also seen those Things in the Holy City of the Supreme Ruler of Great Armies, in the Holy City of our God: because God has Established it Forever. Selah.* Yes, it is a City of Refuge for those Wise People who Humble themselves by Means of Fasting and Praying, until they become like Innocent Children with Pure Minds and Clean Bodies, who Think no Evil Thoughts, who Touch no Unclean Things, who do not Defile themselves with Stinking Painted Skunks, who are Contented with Food and Clothing, who have all Things in Common with the Holy Ones, who Share their Labors for Free: because they Sincerely Believe that **"SWANGKEENOMIKS Rules the Roost!" (HOW all People can Prosper in a RIIT WAA, and Stop Polluting the Earth with Capitalist TRASH!)**, Book 039.

01-03 [ ] *"We have Thought about your Loving Kindness, O God, even while Meditating in the Midst of your Great Temple,* which we have seen Visions of, which will be Built during the Last Days, in Jerusalem, which will be the Headquarters for **'The New RIGHTEOUS One-World Government,'** which will make it Possible for the True Believers to Escape on the Wings of a Great Eagle, you might say, which will Fly Away to Mount Zion, and Land on the Plain of Jordan, where the Giants Live, who are 20 to 30 Feet Tall, who Ride the Woolly Mammoth Elephants, who are their Pets. *According to the Meaning of your Name, O God, so is your Praise unto the Ends of the Earth! Yes, your Right Hand is Full of Righteousness, and your Left Hand is Full of Mercy. Let Mount Zion Rejoice in you, and let the Daughters of Judah be very Glad: beCause of your Judgments.* Indeed, you shall Confound the Worldly-wise People, and bring all of their wisdom to nothing, even as it is written in **"The New MAGNIFIED Version of The Book of MORMON!" (The Story of the White and Dark Indians in the Americas!)**, Book 040.

01-04 [ ] *"Walk all about Mount Zion, O you Scoffers, and go round about her on Horses, if you will. Yes, Count the Watchtowers on the Great Wall, and Understand that no Unclean Thing shall Enter into that Holy City. Yes, Mark you well her Bulwarks in your Minds, and Understand that God Lives in a Mighty FORTRESS: beCause of the many Good Reasons and Great Advantages for doing so. Yes, consider her Great Palaces with Beautiful Stone Dome Homes with Polished Marble Walls, Onyx Tables, Granite Floors, and Agate Windows: so that you might Report it to the Generation of Children who will Follow you: because this God is our God Forever and Ever; and therefore, he will be our Guide, even unto Death."* — NMV of *Psalm 48*.

01-05 [ ] Please Check the following Boxes [ ] with X's, if you Agree with those Statements:

A-[ ] O Selected King, I Agree with the Quotation from the New MAGNIFIED Version (NMV) of *Psalm 48,* which anyone can Read in the *King James Version (KJV)* and all other Versions, and thus Discover that it is telling the Truth of it.

B-[ ] I do NOT Believe it. Indeed, it is nothing but a Religious Fabrication of the Selected King of **The Worldwide People's Revolution!®**, who should be Brought to Court in Shackles and Chains, and made to Prove it.

C-[ ] Can you not Confess that there is ANY Truth in it, O Lady Doubtfulness?

D-[ ] Damn it — it is nothing but a LIE, and so is the Book of MORONS!

E-[ ] Educated People Agree with our Selected King — that the Earth is in Fact, HOLLOW! {See the Internet for the PROOF, and Understand that our Selected King will be Happy to come to Court; but, only IF all of the Leaders of all Nations come to Court with him, whereby he might Ask them Important Questions, and thus Discover the Truth concerning all Important Subjects. Yes, it is called: **"The GREAT Worldwide TELEVISED Court HEARING!" (That Great Meeting of the Most Intelligent and Well-Educated Minds!) By The Worldwide People's Revolution!®** Book 041.}

(HOW the True Church will Escape from the Great Tribulation!)

F-[_] I Fail to Understand WHY we would have to Torment ourselves with any such Great Meeting of the Least Intelligent Minds, when it can easily be Proven that there is NO HOLE at the Pole, much less at the South Pole: beCause Admiral Richard E. Byrd clearly stated: "I went to that Enchanted Land in the Sky, beyond the South Pole." †§‡

G-[_] God Knows the Truth of it, and God has not Spoken to anyone about it. {See www.Amazon.com for: **"God Speaks and the Whole World Listens!" (Fire on the Mountain from the Burning Bush by the Spirit of Truth!) Book 026.**}

H-[_] I Hate to Inform you Silly People that the so-called *Holy Bible* is nothing but Jewish Mythology at its Worst; but, that is the Truth of it: because it is an Invention of Lying Red Jews, who are a Mixture of Edomites and the Tribes of Judah, Levi, and Benjamin, who Hate the Truth about any Subject, who would go to any Amount of Effort that is Necessary to HIDE the Whole Truth, whatever it might be! Yes, have you not "red" **"The Nature of CAPITALISM!" (A List of the EVILS of CAPITALISM!)**, Book 038? Well, it is only Outdone by **"SWANGKEENOMIKS Rules the Roost!" (HOW all People can Prosper in a RIIT WAA, and STOP Polluting the Earth with Capitalist TRASH!)**, Book 030, which should be Carefully Studied by all Honest Environmentalists, who should also Study: **"The Environmentalists' Paradise!" (HOW almost Everyone could be Living in a Beautiful Manmade Paradise!) By The Worldwide People's Revolution!® Book 035.**

I-[_] I Hate to Inform you that I am Intelligent Enough to Spot a SNAKE when I See one, and your Selected King is no Doubt the Most Deceptive LYING Snake who ever Lived, being far Worse than that Lying Joseph Smith Junior, who supposedly Translated *The Book of Mormon* from Sheets of Pure Gold, during the 1800's! †§‡ {See: **"The New MAGNIFIED Version of The Book of MORMON!" (The Story of the White and Dark Indians in the Americas!) By The Worldwide People's Revolution!® Book 040.**}

J-[_] Justice Demands that you Present some Provable Evidence for all such False Accusations: beCause I just Happen to Know that our Selected King is God's Chosen PEACOCK. Yes, he is the Colorful Peacock from Angel Ridge, King's Mountain, Kentucky, United States of North America, who is the Author of more than 350 Inspired Books, which neither you nor anyone else has Proven to be WRong. Otherwise, you would Present some EVIDENCES for Just Judgments. †‡

K-[_] King Jesus will Prove that Ignorant Peacock to be WRong during the Day of Judgment, when he Returns in the Dark Awesome Rolling Clouds of a FEARSOME Sky with all of his Holy Angels, who are NOT 40 Feet Tall, nor is Jesus 400 Feet Tall, as that Lying Peacock has Reported in: **"SWANGKEENOMIKS Rules the Roost!" (How all People can be Greatly Deceived by the Tale of a Lying Peacock and his Rope of Hopelessness!)**, Book 000040000! After all, if there were any Truth in it, the *Bible* would say so. Indeed, it Clearly states that when Jesus Christ Comes the Second Time, that every Eye shall See him, even the Eyes of those People who Pierced his Side and Mocked him while he was Hanging on the Torture Stake. †§‡§§ (See *Revelation whatever*.)

L-[_] Lots of Laughs! HOW could every Eye See him, if he were not a GIANT of a Man in the Sky, Riding on his Great White Horse? Indeed, it is only Reasonable to Think that he is at least 400 Feet Tall, or else the *Holy Bible* is a Jewish Fairy Tale! Therefore, that is all the more Reason for us Education Slaves, Work Slaves, Tax Slaves, Interest Slaves, Insurance Slaves, Drug Slaves, Sex Slaves, Transportation Slaves, ElecTrickery Bills Slaves, Gas Bills Slaves, Food Bills Slaves, Water Bills Slaves, Entertainment Bills Slaves, Repair Bills Slaves, Mortgage Bills Slaves, Childcare Slaves, and Endless Bills Slaves to DEMAND **"The GREAT Worldwide TELEVISED Court HEARING,"** whereby we might Learn the Whole Truth about all such Things — including whether or not Men Landed on the Moon, and whether or not the Evil Events of September 11th, 2001, were Inside Government Covert Operations, called False Flag Operations, or what? Yes, we Need to LEARN THE WHOLE TRUTH, whatever it might be: beCause TRUE JUSTICE DEMANDS IT. In Fact, there is no Way that we can Rest in Peace without True Justice for ALL Peoples, which Balances on **"The Swanky Sword of Divine Truths!"** {See the Sign and Seal of **"The New RIGHTEOUS One-World Government"** on the Front Cover of it, or on the Front Cover of: **"God Speaks and the Whole World Listens!" (Fire on the Mountain from the Burning Bush by the Spirit of Truth!)**, Book 026.}

M-[_] Are you People so Stupid that you cannot Understand that MONEY is the Motive for almost ALL Evils, including the Evil Events of September 11th, 2001, which put TRILLIONS of Dollars into the Hands of Lying Conniving EDOMITES, who were the same Breed of Snakes who Orchestrated the Crucifixion of Jesus Christ, himself, who Called themselves JEWS; but, they were not True Israelites!? {See *Revelation 2:9 and 3:9.*} Indeed, Jesus was an Honest WHITE Judahite, while those Scribes and Pharisees were Lying Hypocrites, which can be Proven in a Courtroom with Law and Order. †§‡ {See: **"Are we Tax Slaves of a Lower Order than those Lying EDOMITES!" (HOW to be Liberated from all Slavery, Worldwide!) By The Worldwide People's Revolution!®** Book 052. See also: **"The Root Cause for almost all Evils!" (The Strange Things that People Say and Do to Get more Money!) By The Worldwide People's Revolution!®**, Book 078, which is a Companion Book of: **"Has your Life become Extremely Complicated?" (HOW to Live a SIMPLE Life!) By The Worldwide People's Revolution!®** Book 068.}

N-[_] Not everyone will Want to Attend that Great Meeting of the Most Intelligent Minds: beCause, if they are Sinners, they will be Afraid of being Proven to be WRong, which will be Easy for your Selected King to Do, if he is in Charge of Things: beCause he is a GENIUS, just in case you have not Noticed it with a Capital N! Yes, he has Written no less than 40 Inspired Books during the past 2 Years, and has often Written one per Week: beCause he has a Special Gift from the Master Farmer, which can easily be Proven in a Courtroom: beCause no one else on this Earth is Able to DO that! Yes, I Challenge you to Discover or Uncover anyone who can Do that, with or without their Black Robes of Hypocrisies and Lies! Indeed, the Supreme Court Justices have been Appointed to their Offices by the Presidents of **"The Divided States of United Lies"**: beCause of Judging them to be the Most Intelligent People in the United States; but, they are all AFRAID of our Selected King, who has the POWER and the GIFTS of GOD, who can Transform Rocks into Pure Gold, Raise Up Dead People — such as President Abraham Lincoln, Thomas Jefferson, Robert E. Lee, Adolf Hitler, and his own Brother Lyle; and also Turn Rivers into BLOOD, O Lady Doubtfulness! {See www.Amazon.com for: **"The Low Court of Supreme Injustices is Brought to Trial!" (Our Elected King Butts Heads** with the United States Supreme Court, with or without their Black Robes of Hypocrisies and Lies!) By The Worldwide People's Revolution!®, Book 011, which is a Companion Book of: "Are Americans the Most STUPID People who ever Lived?" (HOW Working People can PROSPER and Live in PEACE Under the Rulership of a RIGHTEOUS KING!) By The Worldwide People's Revolution!® Book 047.}

O-[_] Oh my God! — has Elijah Actually Returned? Are there no Options to Choose from? Will we have to Give Up our Baal Worshiping, and Deny Buzzeldick the Great? Muslims will not Like that, nor will those Punks in Chicago, who Murder Innocent Children, and thousands of them, Annually. †§‡§§ {See: **"A Sure Cure for GUN VIOLENCE!" (HOW TO STOP GANG WARS and CRIMINAL SHOOTINGS!)**, Book 031, which is a Companion Book of: **"Terrorists Beware that your Days are Numbered!" (HOW to Bring those Terrorist Attacks to a Screeching HALT!) By The Worldwide People's Revolution!®** Book 043.}

P-[_] People should get themselves Prepared for the WORST, if your Selected King is in Fact the Man with the Spirit of Elijah: beCause the Rain is Fixing to STOP; but, I had the Understanding that he is the Reincarnation of King Solomon, himself; and therefore, that Explains WHY he is Able to Write 40 Inspired Books in less than 2 Years, whereby they have become the Best Selling Books in all of History! Indeed, I am going to be Wise for myself, and Obtain my own Personal Hand-carved Leather-bound Editions of ALL of his Inspired Books, even if I have to Make them, myself: beCause they will make Perfect Collector's Items for the Day of Judgment, when God will Open ALL of the Good Books, and say: "Did I not give to you People Fair Warning in *the Book of Revelation* — that all of the Good Books shall be Opened up, whereby you might all be Judged According to your Words and WORKS?" Yes, our Evil Works Testify Against us, O Sinners, and there is no Way around it, except to Cooperate with the Selected King of **The Worldwide People's Revolution!®**, who Proposes a Way of Escape for all True Believers, who will Fly Away on the Wings of a Great Eagle, as *the Book of Revelation* puts it in the GAY King James Version, which is Accurate enough to get the Message Across to whomever has Spiritual Ears that can Hear! See *Revelation 12:14.* †§‡ {See: **"How GAY is GOD?" (Oh the Wonders of it all when it ALL Hangs Out!) By The Worldwide People's Revolution!®** Book 071. Yes, Surprise yourself, O Lady Doubtfulness! GOD is GAY! ‡}

Q-[_] The Great Question is this: **"Will the True Church Accept the Inspired Teachings of our Selected King, and thus Escape from the Great Tribulation?** Or, will they have to go through the Great Tribulation, just to Refine their Minds, and to Purify their Bowels?

R-[_] Jesus Christ is the Truth, the Resurrection, and the Life; and he said nothing about any Colorful Peacock arises to Enlighten our Minds about anything. However, he did Warn us about False Prophets, who would Arise in his Name, and even be Confessing that he is in Fact the Christ, and that we should Follow him in all Ways; but, NOT to the Point that we will Abandon our Beloved Cars, Pickups, Trucks, Tractors, Lawnmowers, Chainsaws, Weed-eaters, Microwave Ovens, and Atomic Power Plants: beCause those are all Blessings from GOD, which you can Read about in *Genesis 2—4,* which tells about that *Garden of Eden,* which had no Abominations in it: beCause the Holy Angel, EDEN, did not Permit any such RADICAL Satanic TRASH to get in there! †§‡§§ {See *Revelation 22:15 and Related Scriptures.* "Sorceries" are Druggeries, whereby all Nations have been Deceived.}

S-[_] Satan has you Deceived, if you Vainly Imagine that there are no Cars in Heaven: beCause there is no Way that God could get around without a Car to Drive. †§‡§§

T-[_] *"Truly, Truly, I say unto thee, Today, that thou shalt be with me in Paradise, some Day: because thou hast Confessed the Truth; but, until then, thou shalt Live in Gehenna, where the Worms and Maggots never Die: because of Eating on Rotting Flesh; and where the Fire is not Quenched: because of Burning Trash, where the Smoke of your Torment shall Arise forever and ever: because a Double-minded Person is Unstable in all of his Ways."* — The Sarcastic Version †§‡

U-[_] I do not Understand all such Words, and I am far too Lazy to Read the *New Testament* with a Capital R. Therefore, I will just have to Live in some Underground Cave, perhaps in the State of Misery, where I can Eat nothing but Magic Mushrooms with Mark Twain, Huck Finn, Tom Sawyer, Aunt Polly, Judge Thatcher, Injun Joe and Nigger Jim. †§‡§§

V-[_] The Victory is to him who Overcomes ALL of his Sins, including his Bad Habits and his Dietary Sins. {See www.Amazon.com for: **"DIETS!" (A Reasonable Solution for the "Eternal Controversy"!) By The Worldwide People's Revolution!® Book 037.**}

W-[_] I would much rather go to WAR, and Kill ISIS (Israeli Secret Instigation Services), rather than Humble myself by Means of Fasting and Praying, like the People of Nineveh did, who Fasted for 40 Days and 40 Consecutive Nights, according to *the Book of Jonah,* which Jesus Referred to as True Repentance in *Matthew 12:40.* Yes, I Know that Jesus also Fasted and Prayed for 40 Days, according to *Matthew 4;* but, it is not Necessary for us to Follow him into the Wilderness with your Selected King, who Fasted for 314 Days during 14 Months: beCause he is a Religious FANATIC, who should be Brought to Court in Shackles and Chains, just for Upsetting our Great False Economy, which was doing Fine, until he came along with his: **"SWANGKEENOMIKS Rules the Roost!" (HOW all People can Prosper in a RIIT WAA, and Stop Polluting the Earth with Capitalist TRASH!)**, Book 039, which will Prove to be the Downfall of Babylon! †§‡§§ {See: **"The Great False Economy is now DEBUNKED!" (Adolf Hitler had a much Better Economic System!) By The Worldwide People's Revolution!®**, Book 053, which is a Companion Book of: **"The UGLY Scarred Dishonest Face of Poor Old Miserable UNCLE SAM!" (A Memorial Day Legacy!) By The Worldwide People's Revolution!® Book 054.**}

X-[_] X-amount of People will say that you are CRAZY: because it would be far Better for us to Humbly Submit to **"The Swanky Sword of Divine Truths!" (The Most Powerful Weapon in the Whole Universe!) By The Worldwide People's Revolution!® Book 067.** Yes, it might be a bit Humiliating; but, at least no one will get KILLED by it. {See www.Amazon.com for: **"WHY do I have to be Surrounded by CRAZY PEOPLE?" (Do almost all People Feel like they are Surrounded by Crazy People??), Book 005.**}

Y-[_] I might have Believed you, Yesterday; but, after Reading the Words of Jesus Christ, I am Convinced that he came to bring DIVISION among us with his own Sword of Truths. Yes, his Inspired Words can easily be Misinterpreted, or else there would not be 400+ Different Major Religions that Profess to Believe in him, and thousands of Minor Sects that Believe otherwise. {See: **"Which Church is the Riit Cherch?"**}

(HOW the True Church will Escape from the Great Tribulation!)

Z-[_] The Great ZEAL of our Selected King will Straighten us Out, if we just Cooperate with him, and DEMAND **"The GREAT Worldwide TELEVISED Court HEARING!" (That Great Meeting of the Most Intelligent and Well-Educated Minds!) By The Worldwide People's Revolution!®** Book 041.

01-06 [_] So, which Boxes did you Check with an X?

01-07 [_] O Selected King, I Checked the Z Box: beCause I Know in my Heart that there is only ONE Rational Way to Solve all such Controversies in a Peaceful Manner, and that is within a COURTROOM, where there is Law and Order, where all Witnesses are Welcome to Testify in Favor of the Truth, whatever it might be. Indeed, I do not Care whether or not YOU are RIIT, nor whether or not they are WRong, just as long as we get to Hear ALL Viewpoints of Honest Righteous People, who can Present their PROOFS. For Example, it will not Require much Time to Prove that the Average American House is a Wooden / Plastic Firetrap Mouse-infested Cockroach Den, which does not Heat nor Cool itself, which is Guaranteed to Rot Down, Burn Up, get Eaten Up by Termites, Flooded Out, Slid Away in a Mudslide, Blown Away in a Wind, Shaken Down in an Earthquake, or otherwise be Destroyed in some other Way: beCause all such Houses are Inventions of the Synagogue of SATAN, who does not give a Damn HOW we are Destroyed, while you Live in a Fireproof, Termite-proof, Hail-proof, Tornado-proof, Paint-proof, Rot-proof, Insurance-proof, Self-air-conditioned, Tax-proof House, O Elected King, which is Worth a thousand Times as much as one of those American Houses, which are Eternal Expenses — Thanks to those Lying Edomite Banksters, who Refuse to even Loan Money for Building GOOD Houses: beCause they stand to Gain TRILLIONS of Dollars from their Interest Slaves, Insurance Slaves, and Tax Slaves: beCause that is the Way that they have Arranged it, which can be Proven in a Courtroom! Guaranteed. ‡

01-08 [_] O Selected King, I must Confess one Thing for Sure, and that is the Fact that you Know HOW to Cut to the Heart of every Problem with your Sharp Sword of Divine Truths. Moreover, if anyone Fails to Check the above Box, and this Box [_], that Person is Suspect of being some Kind of an Enemy, who should be Watched.

01-09 [_] Well, I am Inclined to Agree with you. After all, who could Rightfully Object to everyone Living within those **"Beautiful Swanky PALACES!" (A New Concept in Living Habits — Swanky Palaces for Poor People!) By The Worldwide People's Revolution!®, Book 066,** which is a Companion Book of those: **"GLORIOUS Swanky Hotels Castles and Fortresses!" (Beautiful Planned City States for WISE Intelligent Well-Educated People with Common Sense and Good Understanding!), Book 019?**

01-10 [_] O Selected King, I OBJECT to it, and Strongly so: beCause God Prefers that we all go on Suffering in our Sins, rather than Repent and Forsake them. Yes, he is Determined to let us all Burn in Gehenna, until we REPENT — except that almost no one Knows what it MEANS to Repent! Therefore, will you Please Straighten our Heads Out concerning that Most Important Subject; or, will you Leave us in the Darkness of Ignorance with the Dr. Rev. Billy Graham and the Popes of Rome, who Obviously have no Idea what it MEANS to REPENT? Otherwise, they would STOP Sinning. †§‡ {See: **"Was Billy Graham Greatly Deceived?" (Giving Honor to whom Honor is Due!) By The Worldwide People's Revolution!®** Book 083.}

The Secret City of the Great King!

— Chapter 02 —

What does it MEAN to REPENT?

02-01 [_] O Selected King, if People Actually Knew HOW to Repent, they could STOP Sinning.

02-02 [_] O Selected King, I Checked the above Box with an X: beCause I Agree with it. However, my Naaber sez that shee duz NOT Beeleev it.

02-03 [_] Please Check whichever Boxes below that have Statements that you Agree with:

> A-[_] I Agree that we must not only Ask for Forgiveness of our Sins, which are Transgressions of God's Divine Laws; but, we must also Overcome all of our Sins, in Order to be Saved for Positions within the Kingdom of God.
>
> B-[_] I Believe that I am already Saved and going to Heaven when I Die, even if I Continue to Sin: beCause we are all Sinners, and whoever Denies it is just a Liar. (See *First John 3,* which is telling the Truth about it.)
>
> C-[_] I Confess that I am a Sinner, if the Definition of a Sinner is one who Transgresses or Disobeys the Laws of God — such as the Ten Commandments, or the Teachings of Jesus Christ, who Magnified the Laws of Moses.
>
> D-[_] DUMBmocracy is NOT a Sin.
>
> E-[_] Educated People Know for a Fact that Demon-ocracy is Anti-Christ: beCause it is MOB Rulership — NOT Submission to Jesus Christ.
>
> F-[_] For Example, if you had a Business with a hundred Employees, and you gave to them a VOTE concerning how much Work they should Do, or how much they should be Paid for doing it, or what Quality their Work should be, your Business would Utterly FAIL. Likewise, if you had a dozen Children, and you gave to them a VOTE concerning how much Pie, Cake, Candy, and Iced-cream they should Eat, they would all likely become Sick and Diseased, by Exercising their DUMBmocracy! ‡
>
> G-[_] God Knows that all Adults should be Free to VOTE for whatever they Want, even if they Vote for Government Welfare Checks that Amount to 10 Times as much Money as they Need for Living: beCause that is the Beauty of Democracy! †§‡§§
>
> H-[_] It is not a Sin to Vote for a Righteous King, who might Set the House in Order.
>
> I-[_] Innocent People do not Need a King to Govern them: beCause they Govern themselves. Therefore, Innocent People should not be Taxed to Support Wicked People.

(HOW the True Church will Escape from the Great Tribulation!)

J-[_] Justice Demands that we all Confess ALL of our Sins, even if we have to Dig around in the Garbage Dumps and Trash Dumps, just to Discover those Sins: beCause no Sin will Enter into the Kingdom of the Gods.

K-[_] King Jesus does not Demand that we Overcome ALL of our Sins, just as long as we Confess that he is the KING, Supreme Ruler, and Anointed Savior. Yes, we must Believe that he was Crucified on a Wednesday, Buried at Sunset, and was in the Grave for 3 Jewish Nights and 3 Jewish Days, and Arose from the Dead Saturday Night at Sunset, just as it is written in *Matthew 12:40*. Otherwise, Jesus would be a Liar, just like all of the Preachers and Teachers of False Religions.

L-[_] Lots of Laughs! Jesus Christ was Crucified on a Good Friday, and was only in the Grave for one Day and 2 Nights! Can you not even COUNT? And to Hell with *Matthew 12:40*, which is Irrelevant to us. †§‡

M-[_] I would say that MONEY is the Motive for all of those False Religions, whose Teachers cannot Resist the Temptation of Teaching their Outlandish Lies — such as People going to Heaven when they Die: beCause, with a Bad Attitude like most Professing "Christians" have, they can Abuse the Earth as much as the Capitalists might Want them to, and Vainly Imagine that they are going to Heaven when they Die; and, that they will never See this Earth again, which False Doctrine is Inspired by SATAN, who would have us to Destroy ourselves and the Earth: beCause he is Related with those Lying Conniving Edomite BANKERS, who have Unlimited Amounts of Money for going to War; but, NOTHING for Building those **"GLORIOUS Swanky Hotels Castles and Fortresses,"** which would Solve more than 248 Massive and 5,000+ Minor Problems — such as Traffic Jams, Pollutions, Taxes, Insurance, Drug Abuses, Drug Trafficking, Poverty, Crimes, Illegal Immigrations, Sicknesses, Diseases, Murders, Rapes, Robberies, Stealing, and whatever! Yes, if you can Think of a Problem in this World, the Solution is most likely found in the Construction of Holy Cities for Holy People. {See www.Amazon.com for: **"The Right Design for Living!" (A List of Great Advantages for Building Beautiful Planned City States!) By The Worldwide People's Revolution!®** Book 012.}

N-[_] Not everyone Wants to Live in a Cave House within a Swanky Fortress, even if such Stone Dome Homes have 25 Good Reasons and Great Advantages for Building them, which are Listed in one of your Insane Books: beCause some People like WINDOWS to Look Out of, whereby they can See into their Naaber'z Bathroom Windows, or perhaps Look across the Street and Watch their Naaber'z House Burn Down, or their Children being Shot by Gangsters, or get a really Good Look at the Destruction that is Caused by one of those Lovely Tornadoes or Hurricanes, which God Created for our Entertainments and Benefits: beCause he Knew that Red Jew Insurance Companies Needed more Money, and that Red Jew Bankers could Collect no less than a Trillion Dollars per Year for Interest on Loans, just by Signing Papers with their Scribbled Names, which you cannot even "reed." Yes, God Knew that his Chosen People would be Extremely Poor without Toxic Paints, Solvents, Gasoline, Oil, and GREASE, which keeps the Great False Economy Rolling along Down to Hell, which is the Destination of all Capitalists. {See the above Link for: **"The Nature of CAPITALISM!" (A List of the EVILS of CAPITALISM!) By The Worldwide People's Revolution!®**, which is Headed by the CHIEF Lying Red Jew:

beCause not even he would Want to Live in a Beautiful Swanky PALACE, if it did not have any Windows! See the Vatican Library, or the Main Library in New York City for the Proof. No one can Tolerate any such Places without Windows to Look Out of.} †§‡§§

O-[_] Your Opinion does not Carry any Weight, O Deceiver. Our Selected King has Proposed that EVERY Stone Dome should have a Skylight Vent and Window in it, just to have Indirect Lighting during the Daytime, whereby the Precious Polished Stones and Fine Hand-crafted Furniture cannot be Damaged by Direct Sunlight. Therefore, you Need to Study his Inspired Books more Carefully. Moreover, if you Want to get a GOOD View, and a GLORIOUS View, you will only have to Walk Outside of your Beautiful Stone Dome Home Complex, and take a GOOD LOOK in the Swanky PALACE, which will have Great Stone Walls in many Great Terraces, each of which will be Covered with Beautiful Fruit and Nut Trees, Vegetable and Flower Gardens, and half-dome Stone Entrances to hundreds of Stone Dome Home Complexes. Therefore, if you Live within the 4th Terrace, for Example, you will be able to Look OUT, Down, Across the Valley, and back Up toward the other Stone Terraces with their Vineyards, Orchards, and Gardens, while also Looking Right or Left for a Mile or more, Up or Down the Valley, which will be Filled with Fruit Trees of Various Kinds, Drooping with Sweet Juicy Fruits, as well as Berry Bushes of Various Kinds, which make the Finest of Sweet Juices, which will be like going to Heaven, just to Drink them! Therefore, do not Allow any Unbelief to Dissuade you from Obtaining your own Beautiful Swanky Palace to Live in, O Lady Doubtfulness: beCause you will LOVE it, Guaranteed! {See the Link below for: **"The Environmentalists' Paradise!" (HOW almost Everyone could be Living in a Beautiful Manmade Paradise!) By The Worldwide People's Revolution!®, Book 035,** which is a Companion Book of: **"Beautiful Swanky PALACES!" (A New Concept in Living Habits — Swanky Palaces for Poor People!) By The Worldwide People's Revolution!® Book 066.**}

P-[_] Most People would say that such a Thing is a Nice American DREAM, or Utopian Dreams; but, in Reality, it can never Happen: beCause People like those Lying Edomite Bankers will not Allow it to Happen. Guaranteed. Indeed, no Powerless President can make it Happen: beCause they are all Ruled Over like Puppets on the Strings of Capitalist HOGS! †§‡ {See www.Amazon.com for: **"Mark Twain Races for the PRESIDENCY!" (The 2020 Presidential Candidates Desperately Need Some STRONG Undefeatable COMPETITION!) By The Worldwide People's Revolution!®, Book 033.**}

Q-[_] The Great Question is this: **"Will those Hateful Terrorists not Discover a Way to Infiltrate all such Beautiful Planned City States, and BOMB the Innocent Women and Children with Atomic Bombs?"** {See the above Link for: **"Terrorists Beware that your Days are Numbered!" (HOW to Bring those Terrorist Attacks to a Screeching HALT!) By The Worldwide People's Revolution!®, Book 043.**}

R-[_] Repentance does not Require the Construction of any Buildings: beCause the People of Nineveh Repented According to the Preaching of Jonah, who said: *"Yet 40 Days and Nineveh shall be Overthrown."* Yes, Believe it or not, that was his entire Sermon! Yes, read it for yourself in *the Book of Jonah,* and you will See that I am RIIT! Therefore, being Armed with Information like that, anyone in the World can Repent: beCause no other Explanations are Needed! {See the above Link for: **"The Gospel According to our

Elected King!" (The Good News from the Most Modern Perspective!) By The Worldwide People's Revolution!®, Book 077, which Contains the Complete Sermon of Jonah, which can be Proven in a Courtroom, if anyone Doubts it, which is perhaps the Best Sermon ever Preached, which Jesus gave to a Crowd of People in the Land of Israel, from a Rooftop. Yes, it is most Amazing. You have to Read it for yourself.} †§‡

S-[_] There is no Way on Earth that Sinners can Thoroughly Repent, until they Discover ALL of their Sins, whereby they might have a Chance to Repent of them. Indeed, most Americans are not Aware of how many SINS that they are Committing: beCause the Irreverent LOUDMOUTH Sloth-gut Windbag Hole-in-Thy-Head never Mentioned all such Sins, and does not Know the DEPTH of his own Sins, nor how much Trouble he will be in during the Day of Judgment for Rejecting Provable Truths without any Justified Causes. Yes, you will do Well to Read this Statement once again, O Irreverent SNAKE: because you Wear a Multicolored Coat of Self-deceptions, and Strike at the Colorful Peacock from Angel Ridge with the Poisonous Fangs of Hate and Revenge; but, God will Chop Off your Tale of Lies with one Swift Stroke of his Sword of Truths! †§‡

T-[_] Time will Prove our Selected King to be Correct: because, **"The Swanky Sword of Divine Truths,"** is on his Side, and no one can Rightly Fight Against it and Win: beCause it is Sharp and Powerful. Trust me, *"It is a Fearful Thing to Fall into the Hands of the Living God!"* {See: **"All of the Arguments are in Favor of our Selected King, who has Zero Challengers!" (Before you Attend another Election Deception, you should Carefully Study this Inspired Book with an Honest Open Mind!) By The Worldwide People's Revolution!® Book 085.**}

U-[_] I Understand that our Selected King is NOT God; but, he is Obviously a Servant of God, who has the Wisdom of King Solomon. {See www.Amazon.com for: **"Thu Nq MAGNUFIID Verzhun uv Thu PROVERBZ uv KING SOLUMUN in Plaan Ingglish!" (The Understandable Version of the Famous Proverbs of King Solomon in Plain English!) By The Worldwide People's Revolution!® Book 028.**}

V-[_] Our Selected King has a very Bad VICE, which is Exaggerating the Truth to the Point that everyone can See that he is only being Extremely Sarcastic, which might have the Good Effect of Changing the Minds of Supreme Injustices in the District of Criminals, in Washington; but, it has the very BAD Effect of Turning Off True Christians, who cannot Tolerate the Idea of being Proven to be WRong in every other Sentence: beCause it Eats Out their Hearts, you might say, and Causes them to Repent too much! †§‡§§

W-[_] God Knows that there is no such a Thing as "Thoroughly Repenting": because it is Impossible to Repent for going to War and Murdering Innocent People with Big Bombs, once your Head has been Blasted Away with a Cannon Ball! Indeed, just as the Cannon Ball is being Fired, you might Cry Out to God, and say: "O Go ..." and DIE; and therefore, God could not Forgive you: beCause you did not get to Finish the Sentence, even if you Intended to say: "O God, I am Sorry for all of the Sins that I have Committed, except for going to War: beCause I Know that you are a Man of War, yourself, and I am just Following in your Footsteps to the Cross. (See *Exodus 15:3*.) Yes, Wars are GOOD Things for Entertainment for the Gods, who Delight themselves in Spilled Blood and Stinking Guts, and especially if they are those Wicked Amalekites — none of whom Deserve to Live, even if they are little Babies, which is WHY it is Okay for us to Murder them." †§‡ {See the above Link for: **"Does a Good Soldier have to be a MURDERER?" (Seven Great Swanky Armies of Voluntary Working Soldiers!) By The Worldwide People's Revolution!® Book 027.**}

X-[_] X-amount of People will be Greatly Confused by all such Statements, O Selected King, whereby they will not know which Boxes to Check.

Y-[_] Yeah, I Hear what you are Saying. However, if someone cannot Understand what a Statement is all about, they should be Wise, and NOT Check the Box: beCause, if they Check the Box, they might have to Explain what it Means to them, during the Future, which could Prove to be rather Difficult during the Day of Judgment.

Z-[_] Zebras will have no Idea what you are Saying, O Selected King. Try to make some Sense. Can a Man THOROUGHLY Repent, and thus be Saved for some Position in the Kingdom of God; or, can he be Saved by only Partially Repenting of SOME of his Sins??

02-04 [_] Well, it is written several Times in *the Book of Revelation, "Blest is he who Repents of all of his Sins, and Overcomes them, and Stops Sinning."* Yes, that is what it Means to *"Overcome."* Otherwise, it would have NO Meaning at all.

02-05 [_] O Selected King, if that is what it Means, WHY does it not Read that Way?

02-06 [_] Well, you must Try to Understand that the *Bible* is a Mutilated Book of Books, some of which are only a Chapter or 2 Long. For Example, *the Books of Jonah and Malachi* are only 4 short Chapters Long, in spite of the Fact that Jesus did say: *"... according to the Preaching of Jonah,"* as if he had "red" a whole Sermon, which anyone else could also "reed" at that Time: beCause it was apparently after that Time that it was Mutilated. Whatever the Case, the Sermon cannot be Found in the Bible; but, it can be Found in **"The Gospel According to our Elected King,"** which is the Authorized Version: beCause it is Authenticated by the Great TRUTHS within it, which can be Proven in a Courtroom. †‡

02-07 [_] O Selected King, do you have some Special Authority from God to say such Silly Things? Are you not Aware that there are many Provable Truths that cannot be Found in any *Bible*, nor even in *the Book of MORMON*, which is much more Accurate than the *Bible*, which can be Proven in a Courtroom? †§‡§§ {See www.Amazon.com for: **"The New MAGNIFIED Version of The Book of MORMON!" (The Story of the White and Dark Indians in the Americas!) By The Worldwide People's Revolution!® Book 040.**}

02-08 [_] Well, there might even be a certain Truth in the *Koran / Qur`an,* which is not Found in the *Bible*. However, I have yet to Find it, and no one has ever Pointed it Out to me. However, there are many Verses of Truths within *the Lost Books of the Bible,* and in *the Forgotten Books of Eden,* which can be Proven in a Courtroom to be True, which makes one Wonder WHY those Books were not Included in the *Bible?* Indeed, if someone is Looking for Errors in *Sacred Books,* they only have to Look into the *Unholy Mutilated BIBLE,* in Order to Discover a whole Slough of Errors, beginning in Chapter 1 of *Genesis,* which I have Pointed Out in other Honest Books —

such as: **"LIGHTNING Versus the Lightning Bug!" (HOW almost Everyone can become Moderately RICH, without Telling Any Lies nor Selling Any Trash!)**, Book 001, and: **"WHY are some Preachers so POOR?" (How almost all Preachers could Get Moderately RICH, without Preaching any Outlandish Lies!)**, Book 009.

02-09 [_] O Selected King, in Order to THOROUGHLY Repent, even near unto DEATH, as Omni did, one must Fast and Pray, until one becomes like an Innocent Child with a Pure Mind and a Clean Body, which is WHY King David said: *"I Humbled my Soul by Means of Fasting ..."* — *Psalm 35:13.* Yes, it is written, *"If my People, who are Called by my Name, shall Humble themselves by Means of Fasting and Praying, until they become like Innocent Children with Pure Minds and Clean Bodies, even as the People of Nineveh Humbled themselves, and Seek to have Faces like mine, and Turn Away from all of their Wicked Ways; then I will Hear from the Sky, and will Forgive them of their Sins, and will Heal their Lands, and Cause them to Prosper with True Prosperity."* — *The New MAGNIFIED Version of Second Chronicles 7:14.* †‡

02-10 [_] Well, that is not Exactly what it states; but, it is still the Truth, which makes it Acceptable to God and to all Righteous People, who are not Faultfinders. The Problem with that Statement is the Fact that the People of Nineveh Lived long after the Statement was made; and therefore, it would not be Historically nor Chronologically Correct; but, the Great Truth within the Statement cannot be Rightly Denied, even if the "Setting" is not Accurate.

02-11 [_] So, O Selected King, does God not Care if we tell a few LIES while Telling the Truth?

02-12 [_] Well, if someone got Hypercritical about the Parables of Jesus Christ, that someone could Classify all of his Parables as LIES, even though they are Stuffed with Truths, for Educational Reasons. After all, Jesus was a Teacher, not a Preacher. Indeed, you can read the Parable of the Prodigal Son in my Inspired Book, called: **"SWANGKEENOMIKS Rules the Roost!" (HOW all People can Prosper in a RIIT WAA, and STOP Polluting the Earth with Capitalist TRASH!)**, Book 039, which MAGNIFIES the Parable, and Greatly Improves on it; but, without Destroying any Truth within it, which is Acceptable to the Godkind and to Mankind.

02-13 [_] So, O Selected King, if Fasting and Praying is Necessary for Salvation, what about the Thief on the Cross, who never even had TIME to "Repent," if your Definition is Correct? †‡

02-14 [_] Well, as with most Controversies, you are Speaking about another Subject, while I am Speaking about being Saved for a Position in the Kingdom or Government of God, which is not made Clear within the Mutilated Bible. However, it is an Easy Subject to Understand. Indeed, you probably Remember a certain Verse that states that *"... whosoever calls on the name of the LORD shall be saved."* It should have red, *"... shall be Saved Alive,"* whereby it would not be Implying that everyone who says, "O Lordy, Iiz Bleevz in yu," as "Nigger Jim" might say, will be Saved for a Position in God's Good Government, who probably does Believe in him; but, is he Saved from all of his Sins, and thus Qualified to Rule with Christ in his Holy Kingdom? For Example, George Warmonger Bush and Little Dick Chicanery, Incorporated, had more than a Million People MURDERED by their Armies, by one Means or another, and George Professed to "Believe" in Jesus Christ at the Time; but, did that make him a Saint? Did that Qualify him for a Position in the Government of God? Not hardly. Not at all. In Fact, he was LOST, Confused, and Bound for HELL. Indeed, if he presently Learns this Great Truth, and Wants to be Saved for a Position in the

Government of God, he will have to Confess ALL of his Sins, and Repent like the People of Nineveh Repented, just to be "SAVED." Otherwise, he will likely be Cast OUT, along with his Coconspirators — such as Little Dick Chicanery, Condoosleezee Rice Patty, Paul Wolfwits, and whomever went along with the False Flag Operations of September 11th, 2001! ‡ {See the Internet for www.AE911TRUTH.org which has a Special Enlightening Program called: **Experts Speak Out,** which can also be found on YouTube Videos.}

— Chapter 03 —

How many Different Kinds of Salvations are there??

03-01 [_] If you have "red" the *Bible* more than once or twice from Cover to Cover, you have most likely Noticed that much of it is about as Clear as Muddy Water, which Explains WHY there are 10,000 Different Religious Sects reading the same *Holy Bible,* which is a Disaster for many People, who completely Misunderstand it, who take many Things OUT of Context — such as that Thief on the Cross, to whom Jesus said: *"Truly, I say to you, Today, that you shall be with me in Paradise."* — Luke 23:43, which reads like this in the Gay King James Version: *"And Jesus said unto him, Verily I say unto thee, To day shalt thou be with me in paradise."* And here are some more Versions for you to Study. Please Check the Box by the Statement that you Believe is most Accurate:

    A-[_] And Jesus said to him, "Assuredly, I say to you, today you will be with Me in Paradise." — New King James Version (NKJV)

    B-[_] And Jesus replied, "I assure you, today you will be with me in paradise." — New Living Translation (NLT)

    C-[_] Jesus answered him, "Truly I tell you, today you will be with me in paradise." — New International Version (NIV)

    D-[_] And he said to him, "Truly, I say to you, today you will be with me in Paradise." — English Standard Version (ESV)

    E-[_] And He said to him, "I assure you: Today you will be with Me in paradise." — Holman Christian Standard Bible (HCSB)

    F-[_] And He said to him, "Truly I say to you, today you shall be with Me in Paradise." — New American Standard Bible (NASB)

    G-[_] And Jesus said to him, "I tell you the truth, today you will be with me in paradise." — New English Translation (NET). Please notice that this Translation inserts "the truth," while none of the others do.

    H-[_] And he said to him, "Truly, I say to you, today you will be with me in Paradise." — Revised Standard Version (RSV)

(HOW the True Church will Escape from the Great Tribulation!)

I-[_] And he said unto him, Verily I say unto thee, To-day shalt thou be with me in Paradise. — American Standard Version (ASV). This Version was Translated by someone who Sincerely Believed that there is a Difference between "Today, to day, and To-day," even though no one can Explain what that Difference is to him who Listens to it being "red." Perhaps there is Actually a Top Secret Difference, or a Subtle Difference that I Fail to Understand.

J-[_] and Jesus said to him, 'Verily I say to thee, To-day with me thou shalt be in the paradise.' — Young's Literal Translation (YLT). Note that a Literal Translation would be: and Jesus said to him, "To you I Truly say this Day, in the Paradise you shall be with me." — Master Twain's Literal Translation (MTLT)

K-[_] And Jesus said to him, Verily I say to thee, This day shalt thou be with me in paradise. — Webster's Bible (WEB)

L-[_] Yeshua said to him, "Assuredly I tell you, today you will be with me in Paradise." — Hebrew Names Version (HNV). Note that there are many Controversies over the Correct Names of Jesus, God, and every Character in the entire Bible! Indeed, some People say that we should use the Original Hebrew Names, only: because no one would Want to be called by any Strange Name — such as Jesus, when your Name is Actually Yoshua, which is a fairly Strong Argument. However, the Problem is that no one on this Earth could Know for Sure just HOW his Name is Pronounced, unless they Heard him Speak his Name, and even then they might have Bad Hearing, whereby they could not Hear Subtle Sounds. A Literal Translation of Jesus Christ is Christ Jesus, which is Translated as "the Anointed Savior" in Plain English.

M-[_] And the Anointed Savior said to the Thief on the Torture Stake, "Truly I say to you Today, that you will be with me in Paradise." After all, it was Impossible for the Thief to be with Jesus in Paradise that same Day: beCause Jesus did not Arise from the Dead until 3 Nights and 3 Days LATER, according to *Matthew 12:40.* But, of course, those Words can also be Translated in a hundred Different Ways!

03-02 [_] O Selected King, are you Sure that the SPIRIT of Jesus was not in Paradise that same Day with the Thief? (See *Luke 23:46.*)

03-03 [_] Well, Jesus told Mary to not Touch him: beCause he had not yet Ascended to his Father. (See *John 20:17.*) Therefore, even 3 Days later, he had not yet gone to Paradise. ‡

03-04 [_] O Selected King, I would say that Jesus did not Want to Touch her: beCause of Accepting the Good Advice of the Apostle Paul, who wrote in *First Corinthians 7:1,* "*Now concerning the things whereof ye wrote unto me: It is good for a man not to touch a woman.*" Therefore, he did not Want to Touch her: beCause he had not had Sex in 34 Years. †§‡

03-05 [_] Well, whatever the Case, would Jesus have been Unsaved, if she had Touched him? After all, someone had Touched him when they took him down from the Torture Stake. Moreover, Thomas thrust his Hand into his Side, where the Spear Hole was, some Time later. Therefore, he must have Ascended to his Father between those Times, whereby he must have been made

Immortal; but, nothing in the *Bible* Reveals anything about it: because that is all Top Secret Information. (See *Luke 24:39; John 20:25, and 27; and Acts 1:3.*)

03-06 [_] O Selected King, Noah was Saved from the Great Flood; but, it had nothing to do with his Salvation, did it?

03-07 [_] Well, I suppose that it would Depend on what your Definition of "Salvation" is. Your Question, itself, is Self-contradictory. Noah's Salvation Depended on his WORKS, whereby he Built an Ark. Otherwise, he would not have been Saved from it. The Dictionary defines it as: "deliverance from sin and its consequences, believed by Christians to be brought about by faith in Christ." However, that is not the only *Biblical* Definition of it: because Noah was most Definitely SAVED from the Great Flood, according to the Story, even as Lot and his 2 Daughters were Saved from Sodom and Gomorrah: beCause of OBEYING the Angels; but, that does not Mean that either one of them was Saved for Positions in the Kingdom of God: beCause that is another Subject, which the Bible does not make very Clear, or else someone might Teach something about it, other than myself. Indeed, most of the Teachings of Jesus were about the KINGDOM of GOD, or the KINGDOM of HEAVEN, which is most often Mistranslated. For Example, it should be Translated as, *"The Kingdom that is Coming FROM Heaven, and will be Established on the Earth, ..."* is like this or that: beCause many People Interpret their Bibles to be saying that the Kingdom is IN Heaven, and that we are all going to Heaven to be IN the Kingdom, when, in Fact, the Kingdom is Coming to the Earth: so that God's Will can be Done on the Earth, even as it is Done in Heavenly Places. Yes, here is the Lord's Prayer, just to Prove it:

> A-[_] Therefore, Pray according to this Manner, after you Discover a Peaceful Quiet Place, all alone, to Pray, where you can be alone with God, who is All that is Good:
>
> B-[_] Our Father who is in the Sky, Hallowed is your Holy Name, which is Honored above all other Names in the World.
>
> C-[_] May your Good Government, even your Holy Kingdom, come to the Earth as soon as Possible, and your Will be Done on the Earth, as soon as we Elect a Righteous King to Govern us, even as it is now Done in Heavenly Places.
>
> D-[_] Seeing that we are your Self-disciplined Ones, please Provide for us our Daily Foods, and Help us to Provide others with their Daily Spiritual Foods, if they are Unable to Provide their own.
>
> E-[_] Please Forgive us of our Debts, even as we have Forgiven our Debtors: because we are all Indebted to you for the many Good Things that you have Cheerfully Provided for us; and, if not in Person, then otherwise, by Nature's Blessings, and by the Generosity of whomever might Love us.
>
> F-[_] And, last of all, do not Allow the Devil to Lead us into any more Temptations: because we are already Plagued enough by our own Lusts; but, Deliver us from all Evils, and Especially those that are brought about by our own Ignorance, and by Means of Capitalism, which is the Love of Money in Action: because this is the Devil's Unholy Kingdom; but, yours is the Holy Kingdom, the Power, and the Glory, Forever. Amen. — The Capitalist's Version ‡

03-08 [_] O Selected King, that might be an Appropriate Prayer for one of the Apostles; but, what about us Common People, who have to Work for a Living? Would we not Need a Different Prayer?

03-09 [_] Well, I would say that you would most Definitely Need a Different Prayer. For Example:

A-[_] Therefore, Pray according to this Manner, after you Discover a Peaceful Quiet Place, all alone, where you can Pray in Peace, where you can be alone with God, who is All that is Good:

B-[_] Our Father, who is the Invisible God in the Big Sky above, Hallowed is your Holy Name, which is Honored above all other Names in the World, which is Yohoovu in Funetik Ingglish, and God knows what it is in Hebrew, which is Identified as YHVH, which has no particular Meaning to us Ignorant People. However, we can Accept the Fact that your Name — whatever it might be — must have a Special Meaning, which the Anointed Savior never Mentioned during all of his Ministry; but, he only Referred to you as our Heavenly Father, which is Comforting and Reassuring, seeing that you are the Best of Fathers, and no Warmonger like the Old Testament God, who Commanded Genocide on the Canaanites, Hittites, Hivites, Perizites, Jebuzites, and those Capitalist Niggers like Bernie Madoff, Incorporated, which would Include other Niggers like George Warmonger Bush and Little Dick Chicanery, who should be Exterminated by some Benevolent Plague, if you ever do get around to Executing True Justice for us Tax Slaves. Otherwise, we will have to go on Suffering with their Indignities, as well as those of their Offsprings.

C-[_] May your Good Government, even your Holy Kingdom, come to the Earth as soon as Possible, and your Will be Done on the Earth, as soon as we Elect some Righteous King to Govern us, even as it is now Done in Heavenly Places. After all, we are supposed to have Democracy and Freedom, whereby we can Vote for whomever we Trust, and there is not a more Honest Person on this Earth, that we know of, who has such Reasonable Solutions for our Massive Problems, than the Selected King of **The Worldwide People's Revolution!®** Therefore, Please Help us to Draw our Heads OUT of the Sewage Pipes of Capitalism, and VOTE for The GOAT! {See www.Amazon.com for: **"Mark Twain Races for the PRESIDENCY!" (The 2020 Presidential Candidates Desperately Need Some STRONG Undefeatable COMPETITION!), Book 033, plus: "SWANGKEENOMIKS Rules the Roost!" (HOW all People can Prosper in a RIIT WAA, and STOP Polluting the Earth with Capitalist TRASH!) By The Worldwide People's Revolution!®** Book 039.}

D-[_] O God, seeing that we are not your Self-disciplined Ones, like the Apostles, please Provide us with enough Strength to Provide our Daily Foods, and to Store Up extra Foods for those Old People, Orphans, and whomever is Unable to Help themselves; and also Help us to Provide others with their Daily Spiritual Foods, if they are Unable to Provide their own. After all, some People are so Weak-minded that they cannot even Learn how to "Reed and Riit." Otherwise, they could read **"Thu Nq MAGNUFIID Verzhun uv Thu PROVERBZ uv KING SOLUMUN in Plaan Ingglish!" (The Understandable Version of the Famous Proverbs of King Solomon in Plain English!)**, Book 028, which even Children should be able to Read and Understand.

E-[_] Please Forgive us of our Debts, even as we have Forgiven our Debtors: because we are all Indebted to you for the many Good Things that you have Cheerfully Provided for us; and, if not in Person, then otherwise, by Nature's Blessings, and by the Generosity of whomever might Love us. However, if we Act Wisely, and Establish **"The New RIGHTEOUS One-World Government,"** none of us will have any Debtors: beCause no one will be Borrowing any Money from anyone; but, everyone will become Moderately Rich, just by their Labors, alone: beCause we have many Mechanical Slaves, who can do most of the Difficult Work for us, which Jesus Christ and his Disciples did not have, who were Extremely Poor, who had to Rely on their own Strength to get anything Done: beCause they never Heard of Swanky Land-moving Machines, Rock-cutting Machines, Rock-polishing Machines, let alone Clean Cement Factories and Swanky Concrete Mixers that make a thousand Cubic Meters of Concrete at one Time!

F-[_] And, last of all, do not Allow the Devil to Lead us into any more Silly Temptations: because we are already Plagued enough by our own Lusts; but, Deliver us from all Evils, and Especially those that are brought about by our own Ignorance, and by Means of Capitalism, which is the Love of Money in Action: because this is the Devil's Unholy Kingdom; but, yours is the Holy Kingdom, with the Power, and the Glory, Forever. Amen. — The New Revised Standard All-American Capitalist's Version (NRSAACV)

03-10 [_] O Selected King, I would call that Genuine SALVATION, and Especially if almost everyone in the World becomes Healthy, Wealthy, and WISE: beCause of Studying your Inspired Books. However, I have not even been Able to Persuade School Teachers, Professors, nor Preachers to read your Good Books: because I am not a Good Example for them to Follow. Indeed, I Need to get my own Piano in Tune, you might say, before I will be Able to get them in Tune. In Fact, if I could just get myself SAVED from ALL of my own Sins, I might be Able to Persuade them to Confess their Sins, and even Forsake them. But, being an Unholy Person, myself, HOW can I get them Converted? †§‡

— Chapter 04 —

HOW to get the Nations Converted and SAVED!

04-01 [_] First of all, the Reader must get him or herself Converted and Saved from ALL of his or her own Sins, whereby he or she can be a Good Example for other People to Follow, which is a very "Tall Order," as the Old Saying goes; but, it is the Best Way to Escape from the Great Tribulation: beCause no one is likely to Escape on his own Powers: beCause that Great Eagle that is Referred to in *Revelation 12:14,* can only be Built by United Effort, by the True Church, which will Require Special Skills and a Master Plan: beCause that "Great Eagle" will have to be Large Enough to Contain THOUSANDS of Believers. In Fact, some People would say that it will have to Contain MILLIONS of People: beCause there are Millions of People who Want to ESCAPE by Means of that Great Eagle. Indeed, you likely do not know of anyone who does not Want to Escape, including myself.

04-02 [_] So, O Selected King, why would anyone Want to Escape from this World, if we were all Living in **"Beautiful Swanky PALACES!" (A New Concept in Living Habits — Swanky Palaces for Poor People!) By The Worldwide People's Revolution!® Book 066?**

04-03 [_] Well, right now, the one and only Paradise is Inside of the Hollow Earth, which is where Adam and Eve were Cast Out of. Therefore, it is just Natural that many People would Want to Live in it. {See www.Amazon.com for: **"In thu Beeginingz uv Thingz!" (Thu Kreeaashun Stooree frum thu Beegining!) By The Worldwide People's Revolution!® Book 025.**}

04-04 [_] O Selected King, what we Desperately Need to DO is to get all of the Nations Converted to Jesus Christ, and SAVED from their Sins; and then no one will be Wanting to Escape: beCause there will be no Great Tribulation.

04-05 [_] Well, I am Inclined to Agree with you. However, the "Doomsday" Bible has X-amount of so-called "Prophecies," which would lead any Reader to Believe that whatever Happens is Ordained by God to Happen, and there is nothing that can be Done to Change it in any Way, which is WHY it is Referred to as the "Doomsday Book": because it is all Doom and Gloom, until Jesus Christ Returns to Straighten it Out, which he has had about 2,000 Years to Do; but, behold, nothing has Happened, except that everything is getting Worse and Worse: beCAUSE of Silly Professing "Christians" Believing that Edomite Nonsense, when they could have taken Action a very Long Time Ago to get everyone Converted to the Truth, just by DEMANDING **"The GREAT Worldwide TELEVISED Court HEARING!"** Indeed, there is a certain Clan of Lying Red Jews, who Form the Bad Attitudes of those Professing "Christians," who are like Sheeps, who are called "Sheeple" by their Puppet Masters, who Understand Exactly what they are doing: beCause they Edited the *Holy Bible* to Fit their Agenda, which is to make themselves Richer and Richer, while making the Masses of People into their SLAVES — as in Education Slaves, Work Slaves, Tax Slaves, Interest Slaves, Insurance Slaves, Drug Slaves, College Debt Slaves, Sex Slaves, and Endless Bills Slaves. Yes, the World is Designed by those Lying Edomites for their own Gain, who take Advantage of every Situation that they can: beCause they are Greedy Selfish People, just like Judas Iscariot and Bernie Madoff, who Robbed his Fellow Jews of more than 50 Billion Dollars with a Good Conscience: beCause those Lying Red Jews do not have Consciences! And that is WHY they are called "Psychopaths": beCause they Lack EMPATHY for other People. Moreover, there are many People who Fit into the Psychopathic Category — such as George Warmonger Bush and Little Dick Chicanery, Incorporated, including Henry Kiss-assing-garbage-Desposal-dump, Condosleezy Rice Patty, Donald Rummy Fell, Paul Wolfwits, Larry Silverstinger, Alan Greenspandex, Janet Yeller, Madwoman Albright, and many other Lying Red Jews, who should be brought to COURT for their High Crimes in Low Places. †§‡

04-06 [_] O Selected King, are you not being too Offensive toward all such People? How in the World will you Win their Hearts to Christ by calling them Sleezee Naamz?

04-07 [_] Well, I am much more Worried about the MILLIONS of People who have been Offended by all such Sleazy People, who might have Accepted Christ as their Master and Savior, if such People had not been very Bad Examples of Professing "Christians," whereby they could Murder X-amount of People without it Bothering their Consciences, while bringing about Millions of Refugees! Yes, it all goes back to the Issues of September 11th, 2001, which was a False Flag Operation by the Military Industrial Congressional Bankers' Complex of **"The Divided States of**

United Lies!" (The so-called "United States of North America" in Disguise!), Book 058, which can be Proven in a Courtroom. (See www.AE911TRUTH.org with a Chain of Linking Websites, which Prove that I am Correct.)

04-08 [_] So, O Selected King, it looks like Ike was Riit, huh? Indeed, former President Dwight David Eisenhower WARNED us about that Military Industrial Complex; but, he forgot to Include the Congress and Bankers, who are at the Head of the Snake, along with the Chief Political Puppet, himself, who must Kiss the Asses of those Rich Edomite Bankers: beCause they are in Charge of the Great False Economy, who also LOVE the Second Amendment: beCause it is very Good for those Rich Red Jew Weapons Manufacturers, who can Sell more Weapons. Therefore, ISIS (Israeli Secret Instigation Services) is having a Royal Capitalist FEAST at the Expense of the Extremely Ignorant Sheeple! Yes, every Terrorist Attack puts X-amount of Money into their Pockets: because millions of Frightened Sheeple run out and Buy more Weapons. Moreover, Influential People are even Recommending that their "Students" and Citizens Arm themselves, just in case the Terrorists Attack again, which they are Bound to do: beCause X-amount of them are Muslims, who just Naturally Believe their *Holy Koran / Qur`an,* which clearly states that all "Infidels" — or Unbelievers in Buzzeldick the Great — must be KILLED by whatever Means is Convenient! †§‡

04-09 [_] Well, the Love of Money has Caused many People to Say and Do Strange Things, including arranging False Flag Operations in the Names of Freedom, Liberty, and Justice for all. Therefore, it can be Expected to get Worse and WORSE — unless we, the Masses of People, come to our Riit Senses, and DEMAND **"The GREAT Worldwide TELEVISED Court HEARING,"** whereby we might Learn the Whole Truth, whatever it might be. Yes, I tell HOW in my Inspired Book, called: **"LIGHTNING STRIKES Versus Lightning Bugs!" (HOW you can Become Moderately RICH, without Telling any Lies nor Selling any Trash!) By The Worldwide People's Revolution!® Book 074.** Yes, that is the Easiest Way to get almost everyone Converted to the Truth, whatever it might be: beCause we can Prove those Truths in a Courtroom, and Publish the Information, Worldwide, and in all Major Languages! Therefore, if anyone is Interested in getting anyone and/or everyone, including Red Jews, Converted to Jesus Christ, now is their Golden Opportunity to put their "Best Foot Forward," as the Old Saying goes, and Demonstrate what True Christians are Like — that is, if they are not Spiritual COWARDS, who Want to Run Away and HIDE in the Hollow Earth, which is a bit Ridiculous, I would say: beCause, if there Actually is any Mount Zion, we would have Surely Learned about it from the National Geographic Magazine and NASA, who have lots of Spy Satellites in the Sky. Indeed, *Psalms 9:9, 48, 50, and 87* are Obviously Jewish Mythology. Yes, *Psalm 46:11* clearly states: *"The LORD of Hosts is with us; the Holy City of the God of Jacob is our Refuge. Selah."* †§‡

04-10 [_] O Selected King, that is not a Quotation from any *Bible.* Indeed, you are an Inventor of LIES! God does not have a Holy City, much less a Holy City in the Hollow Earth: beCause the Earth is NOT Hollow! Ask the Trustworthy Federal Government, if you Doubt it. Ask Huck Finn and Nigger Jim, if you Doubt it. Ask anyone with some BRAINS, if you Doubt it. Indeed, there is no Way on Earth that the Earth could be HOLLOW, like your Head, and like your Bones, and like all Heads and all Bones: beCause God would not DO that. In Fact, there are NO Hollow Planets within the whole Universe: beCause I have Visited all of them, and did not Find them. Therefore, it is Impossible, even as any Cantaloupe, Pumpkin, Winter Squash, or Gourd could tell you, if you Cut it in half and took a Good Look at it. God does not make Hollow Things, much less Create Central Suns for all of his Planets: beCause it would Require too much Effort. Besides that, it is just not Logical, if you Think about it; and I have done a LOT of Thinking about it: beCause my Parents Tried to Teach those Lies to me, and the Pastor of our Church also Tried to Stuff our Heads with it; but, I said, "It jus' aant soo: beekawz it woud not bee FEIR." Therefore, there iz no Hollow Earths, nor even Punkinz. †§‡§§

— Chapter 05 —

A Good Heart, but a Bad Head!

05-01 [_] O Selected King of **The Worldwide People's Revolution!**®, whoever made that Previous Ridiculous Statement was Obviously very Sarcastic, and so much so as to Prove herself to be WRong. After all, there are many Naturally Hollow Things in this World of Wonders. Therefore, it is only Reasonable to Think that the Moon was Born from the Earth, whose "Vagina" Naturally Closed Up to some Degree, after the Moon was Born, which would also Explain HOW so many Planets have Moons around them: beCause those Planets also gave Birth to them, which is most Logical and Rational. Therefore, until it is Proven to be otherwise, we might as well Accept the *Biblical* Version of it: beCause it is for Sure that Moses, Elijah, David, Isaiah, and Jesus Christ were much Closer to God than Huck Finn and Nigger Jim, who have never even "red" the Bible from cover to cover so much as one Time: beCause of Judging themselves to be Wiser than Moses, Elijah, David, Isaiah, and the Apostle Paul, who Clearly Stated that he was Caught Up unto the Third Heaven, which is Inside of the Hollow Earth, where the Flying Saucers also come from: beCause more Sightings of UFO's have been Reported from Alaska, than from anywhere else on the Earth: beCause there are Multitudes of Aliens within the Hollow Earth, which "Houses" many Kinds of Aliens, who have come here from many other Planets: beCause the Hollow Earth is an Ideal Place to Live, which is WHY it is called the Paradise with a Capital P in so many Translations of the Holy Bible: beCause it was Understood by the Saints of Old that Mount Zion is Inside of the Hollow Earth, which is why the Psalm clearly states, *"he stretches out the north hole over the empty place, and hangs the earth on nothing." — Job 26:7.* Yes, Uncle Jobe knew about it. †§‡

05-02 [_] O Selected King, why do you Permit such Ignorant Fools to Speak in your Good Books?

05-03 [_] Well, I would not Want anyone to be Falsely Accusing me of not Allowing for Freedom of Speech. {See www.Amazon.com for: **"FREEDOM uv SPEECH!" (U Speshoul Maguzeen uv Onist Upinyunz!) By The Worldwide People's Revolution!® Book 030-0001.**}

05-04 [_] O Selected King, I cannot tell whether or not you are Mocking the Hollow Earth THEORY, or Shining a Bright Light on that Subject?? Indeed, if it is for Real, why does the *Holy Bible* not Clearly say so?

05-05 [_] Well, have you never "red" about *"the Secret Place of the Most High God"*? (See *Psalm 91:1.*) Indeed, if it were not a Secret Place, why would it be called the Secret Place? Try Meditating on *Isaiah 4:5,* and Understand that the Hole in the North is Covered with a Cloud, and the Shining of a Flaming Fire by Night is the Northern Lights! Yes, the Holy City of the Great King is Protected, even as my Inspired Books are Protected by the "Insanities" of them! After all, how can an Unbeliever stand to read all such Literature as this? Therefore, they Mock it, and Drop it. But, Wise People will Remember **"The Seven Basic Spiritual Building Blocks of LIFE!"** (Faith, Hope, Trust, Love, Patience, Persistence and Obedience!) By The Worldwide People's Revolution!®, Book 036, which contains a Marvelous Speech by the Master Farmer, himself.

05-06 [_] O Selected King, you have got to be another Religious MADMAN! After all, in spite of having a Good Heart, you have a very BAD HEAD, which has likely been Warped by all of your own Sarcastic Statements, which have Driven you INSANE! Indeed, there is no Way that God could have a Holy City Inside of the Hollow Earth, and no one Knows about it! †§‡

05-07 [_] Well, I know about it; and there are many other People who also know about it, which can be Proven at **"The GREAT Worldwide TELEVISED Court HEARING!"** (That Great Meeting of the Most Intelligent and Well-Educated Minds!) Book 041. Therefore, if you Want to Learn about it, you will have to do your Best to Spread this Good News: so that many other People might also Learn about, and then DEMAND that Great Meeting of the Most Intelligent Minds! Is that not Reasonable? Is that the Logic of a "MADMAN"? Is that Asking for too much?

05-08 [_] O Selected King, there are a lot of Important Subjects that have Priorities over the Hollow Earth Subject, which could be the Last Thing on the List of Subjects that need to be Proven. After all, there are Billions of People who are Extremely POOR, who do not even have Fresh Clean Air to Breathe, Pure Living Water to Drink, Wholesome Natural Foods to Eat, and Secure Self-air-conditioned Houses to Live in, much less Safe Cities to Live in: beCause there are Potential Terrorists Lurking all about, which Subject you have not even Addressed Properly: beCause you have not told us HOW we can Protect ourselves while we are Building those **"GLORIOUS Swanky Hotels Castles and Fortresses!"** (Beautiful Planned City States for WISE Intelligent Well-Educated People with Common Sense and Good Understanding!) Book 019. †§‡

05-09 [_] Well, I can Afford to Devote the next Chapter to that Subject, since it seems to be most Important to you: because I have nothing Better to Do, Today; but, Tomorrow, I would like to begin **"The New MAGNIFIED Version of The Book of MORMON!"** (The Story of the White and Dark Indians in the Americas!) By The Worldwide People's Revolution!® Book 040. Yes, it has Precedence over this one. However, I would also like to Finish one Book before I Begin another one: beCause that Helps to keep my Thoughts from getting Crossed Over into other Books, even though it really does not matter: because the Important Thing is to get all of my Thoughts Expressed, even if they are all Mixed Up within all of my Inspired Books, just as long as I do not Repeat Things too many Times, whereby some People are Bored by it all, including myself. For Example, Volume 2 of the above mentioned Book contains an Explanation for my Angel Brother Dan, who is Pictured on the Front Cover of: **"Does a Good Soldier have to be a MURDERER?"** (Seven Great Swanky Armies of Voluntary Working Soldiers!) Book 027.

05-10 [_] O Selected King, what you need to do is EDIT all of your Books, and put the Best Parts of them into ONE Large Volume, which would be about as Big as the *Bible,* which People might be Able to Pack to Church with them, in Order to Study the Book with their Friends. However, why would anyone Study such a Book as this, when they have their *Bibles* to Study, which are much Richer, Deeper, Inspiring, and Uplifting? However, we never know when you will Surprise us with a New MAGNIFIED Version of a certain Important *Scripture,* which is very Enlightening to the Mind.

(HOW the True Church will Escape from the Great Tribulation!)

— Chapter 06 —

How to Live in Peace in Spite of Terrorists!

06-01 [_] As much Talk as there is about those Wicked Terrorists, most Americans are in much more Danger of being Murdered by Medical Doctors, who might even have Good Intentions; but, if you are DEAD, what Difference does it make how GOOD their Intentions might be. My Mother used to say that the Road to Hell is Paved with Good Intentions, which seems to be the Truth of it, in spite of not being Found within the *Bible,* which could use a lot of Truths that cannot be Found within it. I Heard a Report on the *Washington Journal,* on the C-SPAN TV Network, which came from a certain Caller, saying that Medical Doctors Murder 800- to 900-thousand Americans each Year from WRong Administrations of MediSINZ. However, I have no Proof of it, and I doubt that he did, either; but, it is frequently mentioned on the major News Networks that 90,000 or more Americans Die in Hospitals each Year from WRong Administrations of Medicines. {See www.Amazon.com for: **"The Washington Journal is a FARCE!" (C-SPAN Managers are not very WISE!) By The Worldwide People's Revolution!® Book 006.**}

06-02 [_] O Selected King, I Recommend that most People AVOID Crowds of People, where there are Greater Chances of becoming Victims of Terrorists, including Public Schools, Universities, Ball Parks, Parades, Marathon Races, Night Shows, Dance Halls, Beer Halls, Churches, Mosques, Synagogues, Temples, Fairs, Rodeos, Court Houses, and wherever People might be Gathered for whatever Reasons: beCause that will Greatly Reduce your Chances of being a Victim of a Terrorist Attack. In Fact, I have Lived my entire Life without being Attacked, just by Following that Rule. †§‡

06-03 [_] Well, your Chances of being a Victim of a Terrorist Attack are much Lower than your Chances of being Struck with Lightning: because very few People are Victims of Terrorist Attacks. In Fact, your Chances of getting Killed in a Car Accident are about 40,000 Times Greater than getting Killed by a Terrorist. Moreover, your Chances of getting Killed by a Gun in your own House are much Greater, which is how most People get Murdered in America, either Deliberately or by Accident. Indeed, some 77,000 or more People Kill themselves in America, each Year, by Overdosing on Drugs: beCause they Obviously cannot See any Good Reason to go on Living, which is an Indication of Bad Health: beCause Healthy People LOVE LIFE, and have no Interest in Dying, and therefore no Interest in Consuming any Drugs of any Kind.

06-04 [_] O Selected King, if that is True, how come George Warmonger Bush and Little Dick Cheney have not Committed Suicide, since they are Mentally SICK?

06-05 [_] Well, they are likely some more "Positive-minded" Americans, who do not Think about their Evil Deeds, whereby they Blank Out their Minds, and thus Live in an American Delusion, even as most Americans do: beCause they cannot Tolerate the Truth about any Subject, much less the Truth about their False Religions and False Economy.

06-06 [_] O Selected King, is it a Lack of Religious Beliefs that make Terrorists so Mean; or, is it because they have too much Faith in some Imaginary God — such as Buzzeldick the Great??

06-07 [_] Well, as a General Rule, when People are very Religious, they are less Harmful. Conversely, the less Religious People are, the more they are Apt to be Harmful. Therefore, it is Safer to Attend Church Services, than to Attend Bars and Dancehalls. However, you must also be Aware that it is Best to keep your own Religious Viewpoints to yourself: beCause some Ignorant People will Want to Murder you for having a Different Viewpoint. Therefore, they are the Extremely Dangerous Kind, who must be Avoided at all Costs, and Especially if they are Radical Muslims, who Sincerely Believe that it is their Duty to Kill any such Infidels as you. ‡

06-08 [_] O Selected King, I Prefer to Carry a Pistol, in Order to Defend myself, whereby my "Peacemaker" will Protect me.

06-09 [_] Well, I can hardly Imagine what Life was like in the Wild West, where almost everyone Carried a Pistol for Personal Protection; but, it must have been a Fearful Time to Live: because everyone was Suspect of Shooting you in the Back, unless they were very Spiritually-minded, which maybe one in a thousand was.

06-10 [_] O Selected King, have you ever Thought of becoming a Terrorist, yourself, seeing that you have Justified Reasons for it?

06-11 [_] Well, I have never Thought of becoming a Terrorist; but, I can Fully Understand WHY many People might Want to: beCause of being Mistreated. After all, I have no Desire to Kill anyone, nor to Die, myself. Moreover, all of my Complaints can be Settled in a Courtroom, Legally. Therefore, it would be rather Stupid of me to become a Terrorist of any Kind.

06-12 [_] So, O Selected King, is it Fair to say that ALL Disputes could be Settled in a Courtroom with a Righteous Judge in Charge of it?

06-13 [_] Well, if a Man and his Wife are both Telling Lies about each other to a Judge, it is Difficult to Prove which one is the Worst of them, unless there are Hidden Video Cameras in every Room of their House, for 24 Hours, 7 Days per Week, until the Truth is Discovered. †‡

06-14 [_] O Selected King, if I were the Judge, I would have them Live with a Christian Family, whereby they might Learn HOW to Live Together in Peace, even if they had to read your New Magnified Version of *First Corinthians 13,* every Day, until they have it Memorized. However, I cannot Recall which Book it is found in.

06-15 [_] Well, you can find it in: **"The Seven Basic Spiritual Building Blocks of LIFE!" (Faith, Hope, Trust, Love, Patience, Persistence and Obedience!) By The Worldwide People's Revolution!®, Book 036, Chapter 04, Verse 10, which Reveals HOW everyone can Live in Peace, in spite of any Potential Terrorists. {See** www.Amazon.com/usa **for: "Are Americans the Most STUPID People who ever Lived?" (HOW Working People can PROSPER and Live in PEACE Under the Rulership of a RIGHTEOUS KING!) By The Worldwide People's Revolution!®, Book 047, which is a Companion Book of: "An Amazing Collection of Wit and Wisdom!" (The Marvelous Tale of the Colorful Peacock from Angel Ridge, and the Strong Rope of Everlasting Hope!) By The Worldwide People's Revolution!® Book 048.}**

(HOW the True Church will Escape from the Great Tribulation!)

— Chapter 07 —

The New Magnified Version of JAMES!

07-01 [_] James, a Humble Honest Servant of Almighty God and of the Supreme Ruler of this World, Jesus Christ, to the Twelve Tribes of Israel, which are scattered abroad — Greetings!

07-02 [_] My Brothers and Sisters, count it as Joy when you Fall into Various Temptations, while knowing this — that the Testing of your Faith Works Patience. Therefore, let Patience have her Perfect Work within each of you: so that you might be Perfected and made Entirely Whole, wanting nothing, even as a Wild Deer is Contented with Food and Fur, you might say: because Major Personal Possessions are Unattractive to True Christians, who have no Ambitions to Own the Mountains, Rivers, Lakes, Oceans, Rainbows, nor Clouds, who are Contented to Live in Beautiful Palaces with other Like-minded Christians, which they all Share with one another. {See www.Amazon.com for: **"SWANGKEENOMIKS Rules the Roost!" (HOW all People can Prosper in a RIIT WAA, and STOP Polluting the Earth with Capitalist TRASH!)**, Book 039, which is a Companion Book of: **"The New MAGNIFIED Version of the Book of ACTS!" (The Understandable Version of the ACTS of the Apostles in Plain English!) By The Worldwide People's Revolution!®** Book 063.}

07-03 [_] If any Man Lacks Wisdom, let him Ask for it from God, who Gives to all Men Liberally, and will not Rebuke you for Asking him. But, when you Ask him, be sure that your Faith is in God, alone, and not in some False Economy; and do not Waver with any Doubts: because he who Wavers is like a Wave of the Sea, which is Driven by the Wind, and Tossed all about like a Drunkard. Indeed, let not that Man Think that he shall Receive anything from the Supreme Ruler.

07-04 [_] A Double-minded Man is Unstable in all of his Ways: beCause he is like the Person who is Attempting to Serve 2 Masters, whereby he is Confused. Therefore, it is much Better for us to Devote our Lives to the Services of God, who asks us to Love our Naaberz as much as we Love ourselves, whereby we are Loving and Serving God. For Example, if each Family has a Different Variety of Fruit Trees, whereby they can Share their Fruits with their Naaberz, it makes all of them Feel Good. For Example, every Tenth House within your Beautiful Planned City State should have a Persimmon Tree, which can be Shared with those 10 Families: so that each Family can have some to Eat. However, if those Families Love those Persimmons, each Family may have a Persimmon Tree, whereby they can Eat them Fresh, and also Dry them, and make what is called "Fruit Leather," which is Chewy Dried Fruits in Thin Sheets, with the Seeds Removed. Likewise, if they Love Figs, each Family should have a Fig Tree or 2, or as many as are Necessary to Satisfy everyone, and also Share any Extra Figs with Visitors, Naaberz, and Distant Relatives, who might not have any to Eat.

07-05 [_] Let the Brother of Low Degree Rejoice in the Fact that he is Qualified to be a Good Servant: beCause, what does a Master Amount to without Good Servants? {See www.Amazon.com for: **"A Sound Argument for Masters and Servants!" (WHY Everyone Needs a Good Master, and every Master Needs Good Obedient Servants!) By The Worldwide People's Revolution!®** Book 008.}

07-06 [_] But, the Rich Person, who has a Higher Degree of Education, should Rejoice in the Fact that he might be Qualified to be a Good Master, who should also be a Good Example for his Servants to Follow and Learn from. After all, whether or not we are Masters or Servants, we are all Subject to Die, even as the Flowers Wither and Fall Off of the Plants, and cannot Save their own Beauty: because the Heat of the Sunlight is Burning Hot on them, and is Bound to Destroy them; and therefore, the Grace and Fashion of it Perishes; and so is the Rich Man and the Poor Man — all being Equal to the Angel of Death, who has no Respect for the Beauty of either one.

07-07 [_] Blest is the Man who Endures Temptations, and does not Yield to them: beCause, when he is Tested to the Maximum Amount, he will Receive a Crown of Everlasting Life, which the Supreme Ruler has Promised to them who Love him and Obey him.

07-08 [_] Let no Man say when he is Tempted, that he was Tempted by God: because God cannot be Tempted, nor does he Tempt any Person; but, every Man is Tempted when he is Drawn Away from God by his own Lusts, or Longing Desires for whatever is Forbidden, and is thus Enticed to Say or Do Evil, which we can Blame on the Devil, who is the Great Tempter and Deceiver. And then, when Lust has Conceived, it brings forth Sin; and Sin, when it has Finished its Destructive Work, brings forth Death.

07-09 [_] Do not Misjudge, my Beloved Brothers. Every Good Gift and every Perfect Gift comes from God, who is All that is Good; and therefore, those Good Gifts come down from the Father of Lights, with whom is no Variableness, neither Shadow of Changing: beCause he is Eternally the same in Nature, and can be Relied on to be Consistent in all Things, being a God of True Justice. However, for the Time being, Satan Governs this World; and therefore, God does not Execute Justice for us, unless we are on God's Side of every Issue, whereby he is like a Defensive Father for us, who will get Revenge for us, if we have been Wronged.

07-10 [_] Of his own Will he Begot us by Means of his Words of Truths: so that we should be a Kind of First Fruits of his Creatures, being True Christians — that is, if we Think and Act like Jesus Christ, who was Devoted to Helping other People, even as a Humble Honest Servant, in spite of being a True Master, who could have Demanded that everyone else should Serve him; but, he did not: beCause he Delighted himself by Helping others, which has a much Better Reward than Serving oneself. {See www.Amazon.com for: **"The Swanky Associations of Working Soldiers!" (A Fascinating Collection of Various Kinds of Voluntary Working Soldiers!) By The Worldwide People's Revolution!® Book 018.**}

07-11 [_] Therefore, my Beloved Brothers, let every Man be Swift to Hear, Slow to Speak, and Slower to get Angry: because the Wrath of Men does not Work the Righteousness of God.

07-12 [_] Therefore, lay aside all Filthiness of Foul Speech, Jokes, and Naughtiness; and Receive with Meekness the Engrafted Words of Provable Truths, which alone are Able to Save your Souls.

07-13 [_] Yes, be you Doers of the Words of Truths, and not just Hearers, only, whereby you Deceive yourselves. Indeed, if any Man is a Hearer of the Words, and not a Doer, he is like a Man who is Beholding his Natural Face in a Mirror: because he Sees himself, and gets a Good Look, and then goes away from the Mirror, and straightway Forgets what Kind of a Man he Saw, who is Far from being a Holy Man like Jesus Christ, Moses, or Elijah.

07-14 [_] But, whoever Looks into the Perfect Law of Liberty, which Liberates everyone who Loves and Obeys the Laws of God, and Continues to Live According to those Laws, he not being a Forgetful Hearer; but, a Doer of the Works of God, this Man shall be Blest by his Good Deeds.

07-15 [_] Moreover, if any Man among you seems to be Religious; but, does not Bridle his own Tongue, and Control his Temper; but, Deceives his own Heart, this Man's Religion is in Vain. Pure Religion, and Undefiled in front of God and the Father of this World is this — to Visit the Fatherless and Widows in their Afflictions, and to keep himself Unspotted from the Vain Things of this World — such as those Stinking Polluting Cars, Vans, Pickups, Trucks, Buses, Airplanes, Lawnmowers, Weed-eaters, Chainsaws, Motorcycles, Motor Scooters, Motorboats, Snow Blowers, Snowmobiles, Garden Tillers, and all such Stinking Noisy Abominations, which are not Required for True Prosperity, much less, Righteousness. {See www.Amazon.com for: **"The Nature of CAPITALISM!" (A List of the EVILS of CAPITALISM!)**, Book 038, plus: **"The Environmentalists' Paradise!" (HOW almost Everyone could be Living in a Beautiful Manmade Paradise!)**, Book 035, plus: **"SWANGKEENOMIKS Rules the Roost!" (HOW all People can Prosper in a RIIT WAA, and STOP Polluting the Earth with Capitalist TRASH!)**, Book 039, plus: **"The Right Design for Living!" (A List of Great Advantages for Building Beautiful Planned City States!)**, Book 012, plus: **"Poverty Hunger Riots Strikes Brutalities Election Deceptions and Civil Wars!" (The High Price that we Earthlings have Paid for Leaving the Good Land!)**, Book 014, plus: **"Seven Great Armies of Working Soldiers!" (HOW to Provide a Way for Everyone to WORK: so as to Eliminate Poverty, Crimes, Drug Abuses, Prisons and Unnecessary Taxes!)**, Book 015, plus: **"GLORIOUS Swanky Hotels Castles and Fortresses!" (Beautiful Planned City States for WISE Intelligent Well-Educated People with Common Sense and Good Understanding!)**, Book 019, plus: **"The CONSTITUTION for the New RIGHTEOUS One-World GovernMINT!" (How all Peoples can get True Justice, and Celebrate the Great Year of JUBILEE!)**, Book 016, plus: **"The Great World TEMPLE of PEACE!" (The Glory of Jerusalem Arises Again!) By The Worldwide People's Revolution!®** Book 017.}

07-16 [_] My Brothers, do not have the Faith of our Supreme Ruler, Jesus Christ, even the Ruler of Glory, with Respect of Persons, whereby you Favor one over another, just because of his or her Looks, Money, Property, Intelligence, Education, Class, Prosperity, Popularity, or Body Build: because, if there comes someone into your Assembly with a Diamond Gold Ring, and dressed in Expensive Clothing; and there also comes in a Beggar dressed in Rags; and you have Respect to him who wears the Delicate Clothing, and you say to him: "Please sit over here on this Soft Seat," while you say to the Beggar, "Stand over there in the Corner, or sit over there on the Floor with the Dog," are you not showing Partiality? Are you not Bias? Are you not Prejudice? Is that something that you would Want other People to say to you, if you were Poor? Have you not become Judges with Evil Thoughts? In Deed, you have.

07-17 [_] Listen to me, my Beloved Brothers and Sisters, has God not Chosen the Honest and Humble Poor People of this World, who are Rich with Faith and Good Works, who are Heirs of his Holy Kingdom, which he has Promised to them who Love him and Obey his Commandments from the Heart, who Treat all People Fairly and Justly, and do unto others as they would have others do unto them? But, you have Despised the Poor People for their Poverty, as if it were not Possible for you to also become Poor and Miserable, and even in a Worse Condition than those whom you Despise, or Look Down on as the Scum of the Earth. Do Rich People not Oppress you, and take Advantage of you in every Way Possible? Do they not Haul you into Courtrooms with their Lawsuits, and do whatever they can to make Life Miserable for you? Do Rich Bankers not Rob you by Means of Usury? Do Politicians not Lie you, and make False Promises to you, and also Favor Rich Hogs and Painted Skunks and Colorful Snakes? Do they not Blaspheme that Worthy Name by which you are Called, and use his Name in Vain with Cursing? Therefore, how can you Respect such People, much less Favor them?

07-18 [_] Therefore, if you Fulfill the Royal Law according to the *Scriptures,* you shall Love your Poor Naaberz az much az you Love yourselves, and thus do Well; and therefore, you should use your Wealth to Provide the Necessary Tools for Assisting your Poor Naaberz to Prosper on the Land: because all Good Material Things come from the Land, which can be made much more Productive than it presently is, just by Adding the Correct Amounts of Powdered Rocks to the Topsoil, which will Feed the Microorganisms, which will Feed the Fruit and Nut Trees, which will Feed whomever gets to Harvest them, which must be Protected by Tall Strong Stone Walls, which will Keep Out all of the Unwanted Varmints, Thieves, Rapists, Robbers, and whomever or whatever might Harm you, which is Ancient Nolij. But, if you have Respect to "Special" Persons, you Commit Sins, and are Convicted by the Law as Transgressors: because, whosoever shall Keep the whole Law, and yet Offend in just one Point, he is Guilty of Transgressing all of the Laws, which are Linked Together like a Chain, which Connects us to God.

07-19 [_] Indeed, he who said, "Do not Commit Adultery," also said: "Do not Steal." Therefore, if you do not Commit Adultery; but, you Murder someone, you are most Certainly Guilty of Transgressing the Laws of God, even if you Murder other People Indirectly: because there are many Ways to Murder other People, and all of them are Evil Ways, which Separate you from the Love of God, who would never Say nor Do anything to Murder anyone. For Example, it will come to pass during the Last Days, during the Days of Wickedness and Revenge, that Multitudes of Ignorant People will be Polluting their Air, Water, Land, Animals, and themselves with their Stinking Noisy Polluting Abominations: beCause of having the Spirit of a Murderer, even without Knowing it, nor Realizing it after being Reproved for it; but, God will Hold them Accountable for it: beCause Murder is still Murder, no matter how one goes about doing it, even Collectively as a Murderous Army. {See www.Amazon.com for: **"The Nature of CAPITALISM!" (A List of the EVILS of CAPITALISM!) By The Worldwide People's Revolution!® Book 038.**}

07-20 [_] Therefore, Speak and Do those Things that are Good, even as if you shall be Judged by the Law of Liberty, which Liberates everyone who Loves and Obeys it: because he shall have Judgment without Mercy, who has shown no Mercy; and Mercy Rejoices against Judgment, even as Peace Rejoices with Victory over War, which is the Most Hateful Thing in the World, whereby Healthy Young Men are Slaughtered like Hogs, and Butchered like Chickens in Vain: because all Disputes can be Legally and Rightfully Settled in Courtrooms, even if a few Sacrifices must be made to Appease the Selfish Greedy Aggressors. ‡

07-21 [_] What does it Profit, my Brothers, though a Man say that he has Faith; but, does not have the Works to Prove it? Can Faith alone Save him from the Burning House of Lies? No, not by any Means: because he must get himself Up and Flee from such a Burning House, just to Save himself by his Works, even as Noah Saved himself from the Great Flood by his Good Works. Likewise, if a Brother or Sister is Naked and Destitute of Daily Foods, and one of you say to him or her: "Depart in Peace, be you Warmed by the Chilly Wind, and Filled with the Bark from Pine Trees," will that

(HOW the True Church will Escape from the Great Tribulation!)

Satisfy his or her Soul? Would it Satisfy you, if you were Naked and Homeless? Notwithstanding, many of you give such Insults to all such Poor Souls, who are in Need of the Basic Necessities of Life, while you Live in Luxuries like Royalties. Therefore, what does it Profit you in the Eyes of God, who is the Final Judge, who will Reward you Justly during the Next Life, when you too may be Born into a Family of Beggars? Indeed, have you Thought about that, O you Greedy Selfish People? Well, if not, how is the Time to Meditate on it: beCause your Days are Limited.

07-22 [_] Even so is Faith, if it has not Good Works to Follow it, it is Dead, being alone, being Powerless to Save you. Therefore, Faith Requires Positive Actions. Yes, a Man might say, "You have Faith; but, I have Good Works. Show to me your Faith without your Works, and I will Show to you my Faith by my Good Works."

07-23 [_] You say that you Believe that there is only ONE God; but, you have no Proof of it: beCause each World Needs a God or Supreme Ruler to Govern it; and therefore, there are many Gods, even if some Lady Doubtfulness Denies it: beCause the Vast Universe is far too Populated and Complicated for any one God to Manage it. Nevertheless, you do Well to Believe in God; but, the Demons also Believe, and Tremble: because they Know that their Judgment Day is Coming, and it Frightens them to the Core of their Souls. Likewise, your Judgment Day is also Coming, and you will be Judged According to your Words and Works. Therefore, if you have Contaminated the Earth with Abominations, you will be Judged for it: beCause this Earth is our Eternal Home, which we should Love and Respect and Care for: beCause it Cares for us.

07-24 [_] But, I want you to Understand this, O Vain Man, that Faith without Good Works is DEAD! And Faith with Evil Works is DAMNED to Hell with Satan and all of his Demon Spirits!

07-25 [_] Was not our Father Abraham Justified by his Works, when he had Offered his Son Isaac on the Altar, whereby he Obeyed God? Do you see how Faith Worked with his Works? and by his Works was Faith made Perfect. And thus the *Scripture* was Fulfilled, which says: "Abraham Believed God, and it was Imputed unto him for Righteousness"; and therefore, he was called the Friend of that Insane Hebrew God, who should have never been Demanding any such Sacrifices — except that the Law of Justice Required it of him. Yes, the Penalty and Punishment for Sins had to be Appeased by the Sacrifices of Innocent Souls, if you can Believe it, which makes about as much Sense as Sacrificing an Innocent Baby for the Sins of his Uncle Sam, which is Ridiculous, if not Totally Insane. Nevertheless, that is the Reasoning of the Hebrew God, they say; but, I say that it was all an Invention of Satan, the Devil, the Great Deceiver, who would have you to Believe that someone else could Atone for your Sins. †§‡

07-26 [_] Yes, True Justice Demands that every Person should be Punished for his or her own Sins. However, the Son of God, being the Father of us all, who brought about the Fall of Mankind when he was Adam, himself, could Atone for the Sins of all of Mankind, if he were Sacrificed for Mankind: beCause he Caused the Fall, whereby he would be Receiving a Just Punishment for his Original Sin, which would also Appease the Wrath of God against Mankind, whereby all People might be Saved, if they Believed in the Son of God, and also Loved and Obeyed him as the Perfected Adam. Therefore, you can now see how that by Works a Man is Justified, and not by Faith, only. Indeed, Faith and Good Works must Work Together, Hand in Hand, and Head with Heart, even as one Body with one Mind, which is the Beauty of **"Seven Great Armies of Working Soldiers,"** who will Accomplish Great Things by United Effort.

07-27 [_] Likewise, Rahab the Harlot was also Justified by Works, in spite of being a Betrayer of Trust, who Betrayed her own People, who had Betrayed her by not Establishing a Righteous GovernMint, whereby she was Forced to Prostitute herself, just to Earn a Living; and therefore, when she had Received the Israelite Spies, she Hid them, and then sent them out by another Way: because she Loved them as Real Men.

07-28 [_] Therefore, as the Body without the Spirit is Dead, so Faith without Works is also Dead.

07-29 [_] Therefore, let your Faith Inspire you to Say and Do GOOD Works, which will Glorify God and Uplift Mankind, and make this a much Better World for everyone to Live in. Yes, Learn to Work Together like a Great Army of Working Soldiers, who Understand that Great Things can be Accomplished by United Effort and Brotherly Love, while nothing Good nor Honorable can be Accomplished by Greed and Selfishness as Independent Jackasses. Yes, Try to Understand that every Servant Needs a Good Master with a Good Plan to Follow, and every Master Needs Good Servants to Help him to Carry Out those Plans. {See www.Amazon.com for: **"A Sound Argument for Masters and Servants!" (WHY Everyone Needs a Good Master, and every Master Needs Good Obedient Servants!) By The Worldwide People's Revolution!® Book 008.**}

07-30 [_] My Brothers, do not make yourselves into many Masters, knowing that we will Receive the Greater Condemnation, if we do not Live Up to our Calling as Good Masters: beCause nothing is much Worse than Bad Masters, not to Mention Mean and Hateful Masters, who will Receive the Greatest Condemnation: because, in many Things we are prone to Offend everyone; but, if any Man does not Offend in Word, nor in Deed, the same is a Perfect Man, and is also Able to Bridle or Control his whole Body and Mind, whereby he makes Good Judgments, and does the Right Thing every Time, even if only to Keep Silent in the Presence of Satan, who is the Chief Ruler of this World, which is in his Domain for the Present Time; but, not for ever: beCause the Kingdom of God will be Established during the Last Days, after People have Suffered Enough to come to their Right Senses, whereby they will Agree that it is Best for them to SEPARATE themselves from the Wicked People, and Establish **"The New RIGHTEOUS One-World Government!" (HOW to Establish a Righteous One-World Government without Going to WAR!) By The Worldwide People's Revolution!® Book 056.** Yes, each Potential Elected King and Queen will Fill Out and File on the Internet **"The Complete SURVEYS of our VALUES!" (SURVEYS of Religious Spiritual Political Governmental Sexual Social Moral Economic Business Labor Habitual and Miscellaneous VALUES!) By The Worldwide People's Revolution!®, Book 059**, whereby the Electors can Study those Surveys of their Potential Leaders, and thus Rightly Judge WHO is most Qualified to Govern them, which will Eliminate those Election Deceptions, and also Save Trillions of Dollars on Political Nonsense! ‡

07-31 [_] Behold, we put Bits in the Horses' Mouths, so that they might Learn to Obey us; and thus we Turn about their whole Bodies by their Bridles. Also, behold the Ships in the Sea, which, in spite of being so Great, and are Driven about by Fierce Winds; and yet they are Turned about with very Small Helms, wherever the Governors Desire to go, if those Ships are not Wrecked against the Rocks, or Broken into Pieces by the Powerful Waves: beCause of being too Big to Manage Correctly, even as a Large Nation finds it Difficult to Manage itself, which should be Divided into Beautiful Planned City States that are Manageable and Controllable by just one Righteous King or Holy Queen, who does what is Riit for all of the People. Even so, the Tongue is a little Member of the Body, and the Voice Box Boasts of Doing Great Things, if you allow it to; but, he who keeps his Lips Closed in the Presence of Ignorant Fools is Wiser than most People: because that is what God does almost all of the Time: because he Knows for a Fact that most Ears are Filled with the Wax of Unbelief; and therefore, they cannot Hear the Pure Truth about any given Subject, whereby they might be Liberated from the Prison of Lies, which is Kept Locked by our Lusts, Selfishness, and Greed, which is Understood by Innocent Children, who have no such Lusts, Selfishness, nor Greed, who are not Self-defensive, nor Aggressive, who are Contented with Food and Clothing while Living in those **"Beautiful Swanky PALACES!" (A New Concept in Living Habits — Swanky Palaces for Poor People!)**, Book 066: beCause almost all Poverty in this World of Woes is brought about by the Desire to OWN Things: beCause of being Possession Worshipers, when no such Personal Possessions are Necessary for True Prosperity, even as Kings and Queens and Popes Live in Palaces that they do not Own. Likewise, all of the People can Live in Palaces that they do not Own, whereby they are Liberated from Education Slavery, Work Slavery, Tax Slavery, Insurance Slavery, Usury Slavery, ElecTrickery Bills Slavery, Gas Bills Slavery, Food Bills Slavery, Water Bills Slavery, and Endless Bills Slavery: beCause of Inventing Mechanical Slaves, which can do most of the Work for them. Selah.

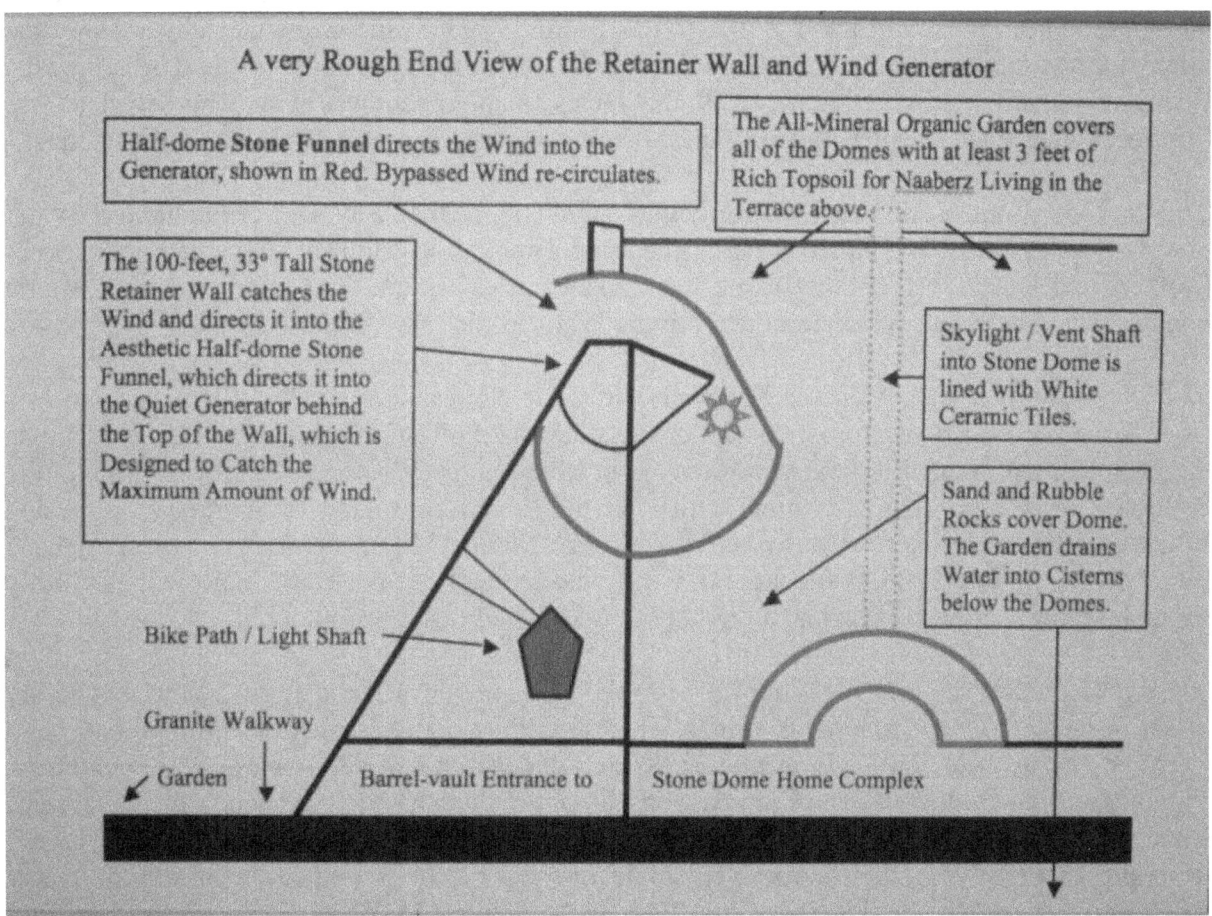

07-32 [_] Behold how Great a Matter a Little Fire can Kindle! And the Tongue is like a Fire, even a World of Iniquity, you might say; and so is the Tongue among our Members, so that it Defiles the whole Body, and Sets on Fire the Course of Nature, whereby whole Nations are Carefully Led Down to Hell by the Inspiration of Satan, who Inspires Foolish Men to be Greedy and Selfish, which Breeds more Greed and Selfishness and Cruelties, which Leads to Hateful Wars, Famines,

Plagues, and Countless Deaths — all for that Edomite Ownership Nonsense! However, the Tongues of the Righteous Ones will Inspire People to Say and Do Good Things, whereby they will Focus their Energies on the Construction of Beautiful Planned City States, whereby everyone can become Moderately Rich, and thus have no Lack of any Good Things, with only an Average of 4 Hours of Common Skilled Labor per Day, or 8 Hours Today, and Tomorrow Off, or this Week On and next Week Off: beCause of being Flexible and Cooperative. ‡

07-33 [_] Are you Aware that almost every Kind of Beast, Bird, and even Serpents and Creatures in the Seas, have been Tamed and Domesticated by Mankind? But, the Tongue of an Unclean Person cannot be Tamed without much Fasting and Praying: because it is an Unruly Evil Thing, you might say, being Full of Deadly Poisons, like the Head of a Snake with Poisonous Fangs. Indeed, therewith we Bless God, even the Father of our Supreme Ruler, Jesus Christ; and therewith we Curse Men for their Wickedness, who were Created in the Image of the Son of God, who must be Converted by the Sword of Truths, which must be Spoken with Love and Affection, in Order to be most Effective, whereby a Cold Icy Hard Heart can be Melted with the Warmth of Love and Affection, which also Requires Good Deeds, which is WHY Moses Commanded us to Feed our Enemies; and, if they are Thirsty, to give to them some Sweet Fruit Juices, whereby some of the Sticky Filth within their Bowels might be Washed Out, whereby their Natures might be somewhat Changed by it. After all, it is that very Filth that Gives Satan Power Over them, whereby they Lose Control of their own Tongues. Indeed, out of the same Mouth proceeds Blessings and Cursings.

07-34 [_] My Brothers and Sisters, those Things should not be that Way. Does a Fountain of Water send forth both Sweet and Bitter Water at the same Time, all in one Day? Can the Fig Tree, my Brothers and Sisters, bear Bitter Olives and Chokecherries? Can a Grapevine bear Figs? Can a Fountain yield both Salt Water and Fresh Living Water at the same Watering Hole?

07-35 [_] Who is a Wise Man and Endowed with True Nolij among you? Let him show to us a Good Example for Living from a Good Conversation that Follows his Good Works, whereby he might Speak with Authority and with Meekness, which is his Wisdom, whereby he might Win Souls to Christ, who Taught nothing, until after he Proved himself to be Worthy by his Good Works as a House Builder, whereby he Spoke from a Mature Mind, and not as an Inexperienced Boy, who has no Practical Experiences in Living, who cannot be Expected to Speak with Authority about anything: beCause of having an Immature Mind, Body, and Spirit.

07-36 [_] However, if you have Bitter Envying and Strife in your Hearts, do not Accept any Glory for it: because those are Shameful Things. Therefore, do not Lie against the Truth, whatever it might be: because you will be Proven to be WRong. Indeed, that Wisdom does not Descend from above, from the Gods; but, it is Earthly, Sensual, and Devilish. Yes, you Know it is: because, wherever Envy and Strife are, there is Confusion and every Evil Work; but, the Wisdom that comes from above is first Pure, then Peaceable, Gentle, and Easy to be Entreated, being Full of Mercy and Good Fruits, without Partiality, and without Hypocrisy. And the Seeds of the Fruits of Righteousness are Sown in Peace by them who make Peace, which Seeds must also be Watered, Weeded, Cultivated, and Cared for with Love, Patience, and Persistence, which every Good Gardener Knows by Experience.

07-37 [_] Where do Wars and Fightings come from among you? Do they not come from your own Lusts, which War in your own Minds? Indeed, you Lust after Things that are not your own, which you did not Earn by any Right by Working for those Things. You Kill other People, and even Murder Innocent Souls, in Order to Obtain their Possessions; and you Desire to have Things that you have no Right to have, and cannot Legally Obtain. You Fight and War, yet you have not those Good Things that you Need: beCause you do not Ask your Heavenly Father for the Wisdom to Obtain the Correct Tools to Work with, whereby you might Prosper in a Righteous Way, and without going to War. Moreover, even if you do Ask God for something, it is to consume it on your own Lusts, rather than Think of all of the Multitudes of Poor People in this World of Woes.

07-38 [_] O you Adulterers and Adulteresses, do you not know that the Friendship of the World makes you an Enemy of God? Whosoever therefore will be a Friend of the Evil Things of the World is an Enemy of God. Do you Think that the *Scripture* says in Vain, that the Evil Spirit that Lives within us Longs to Envy other People for their Gifts? But, God Gives more Grace, whereby we can Overcome the Spirit of Envy. Therefore, he says: *"God Resists the Proud People, and Gives Grace to the Humble, Honest People."*

07-39 [_] Therefore, Submit yourselves to God. Resist the Devil, and he will Flee from you. Draw Near to God, and he will Draw Near to you. Cleanse your Hands, O you Sinners; and Purify your Hearts, O you Double-minded Sinners. Be Afflicted, and Mourn, and Weep, and Howl for the Miseries that shall come upon you, if you do not Repent. Yes, let your Laughter be turned into Mourning, and your Joy into Heaviness. Humble yourselves by Means of Fasting and Praying in the Sight of the Supreme Ruler, and he will Lift you Up.

07-40 [_] Speak not Evil one of another, Brothers and Sisters: because, he who Speaks Evil of his Brother or Sister, and Condemns them, Speaks Evil of the Law, and Condemns the Law; but, if you Condemn the Law, you are not a Doer of the Law, but a Judge. There is one Lawgiver, who is able to Save and to Destroy. Therefore, who are you to be Judging and Condemning others?

07-41 [_] Go to Work right now, at Home, on the Land, you who say: "Today or Tomorrow we will go into such and such a City, and continue there for a Year or so, and Buy and Sell Goods, and get Gain: because you have much Work to Do at Home, without Wandering into some City of Confusion, which is Designed by Satan and Sons, Incorporated, whereby you will only become Poorer and Poorer. Besides that, you do not know what a Day might bring forth, much less another Year. However, what is your Life, if not just a Vapor of Steam, which Appears for a little Time, and then it Vanishes Away? Therefore, while you still have Strength, Try to Say and Do Good Things, whereby you might Improve the World.

07-42 [_] Indeed, you ought to say, "If the Supreme Ruler is Willing, we shall Live, and do this or that." But, now you Rejoice in your Vain Boastings, without knowing that all such Rejoicing is Evil: because your Days are Numbered. **Therefore, to him who Knows to Do Good, and he does not Do it, to him it is a Sin.**

07-43 [_] Go to Bed now, you Rich Men — Weep and Howl for the Miseries that shall come upon you. Yes, your Riches will become Corrupted, and your Garments Moth-eaten. Indeed, your Silver is already Tarnished, and your Gold will not always Shine; and the Rust of your other Metals shall be a Witness against you, and shall Eat your Flesh, as if it were Fire, you might say. Yes, you have Heaped Up Treasures Together for the Last Days of your Lives, as if you could Buy Good Health, once you become Old and Full of Sores and Pains.

07-44 [_] Behold, the Wages of the Hired Laborers, who have Reaped the Harvests of your Fields, which is of you kept back from them by Fraud, Cries Out against you; and the Cries of them who have Reaped are Entered into the Ears of him who Listens in Secret, whose Holy Angels Record all of your Evil Deeds and Hateful Words. Yes, the Ruler of Great Armies will Rise Up Against you: because you have Lived in Pleasures on the Earth, and have been Wanton; you have Nourished your Bowels, as during a Day of Slaughter, when you must Eat the Flesh before it Rots in the Heat. You have Condemned and Killed the Just One; and he does not Resist you.

07-45 [_] Therefore, be Patient, my Brothers and Sisters, until the Second Coming of the Supreme Ruler. Behold, the Husbandman Patiently Waits for the Precious Fruits of the Earth, and has very Long Patience for it, until he Receives the Early and Latter Rains. Therefore, be you also Patient; and Establish your Hearts with True Love: because the Coming of the Supreme Ruler Draws Nearer and Nearer, even though it is still a Long Ways Off.

07-46 [_] Do not Hold Grudges against one another, Brothers, lest you be Condemned. Behold, the Supreme Judge is Standing in front of the Door of Confession, waiting for you to Confess your own Sins.

07-47 [_] Accept our Brothers, the Prophets, who have Spoken in the Name of the Ruler, for an Example of Suffering Afflictions, and of Patience, who Endured the Worst of Cruelties. Behold, we Count them Happy who Endured to the End of their Lives, and did not Deny the God of True Justice, who will get his Justice during the Next Life, after all of the Spirits have been Tested in the Furnace of Afflictions. You have Heard of the Patience of Jobe, and have seen the End of his Life, who Feared the Supreme Ruler — that he is full of Pity, and of Tender Mercies.

07-48 [_] But, above all Things, my Brothers, Swear not — neither by Heaven, nor by the Earth, nor by any other Oath; but, let your Yes Mean YES; and your No Mean NO, lest you Fall into Condemnation.

07-49 [_] Are any People among you Afflicted with Diseases? Let them Fast and Pray, whereby their Strength will be Renewed. Yes, their Flesh will become as Fresh as the Flesh of a Child; and they shall Return to the Days of their Youthfulness, when they could Run all Day, and not be Weary; and they could Walk all Night and not Faint: because they shall be Regenerated by Fasting and Praying, combined with certain Days of Feasting on Sweet Juicy Fruits between all such Fastings. {See: **"HOW to Become a HOLY Man!" (40 Good Reasons WHY People Should FAST and PRAY!), Book 045, which is a Companion Book of: "The Proper RULES for FASTING!" (The Complete Instruction Manual for True Repentance!) By The Worldwide People's Revolution!® Book 046.**}

07-50 [_] Are any People among you Merry? Let them Sing Psalms, while Understanding that most Hymns are Perverted, and do not Reflect the Whole Truth by any Means. In Fact, some Songs are nothing but Outlandish LIES from the Beginnings to the Ends of them: beCause they are Inventions of Satan, the Devil, who would have People to Believe that they are going to Heaven when they Die, in spite of being in their own Manmade Hell, right now.

07-51 [_] Is any Person Sick among you? Let him Call for the Elders of the Church; and let them Pray over him, while Anointing him with Oil in the Name of the Savior: because such a Person has Failed to Study: **"Did God or Satan Ordain Medical Doctors??" (Ask Huck Finn and/or Nigger Jim: because neither Tom Sawyer nor Judge Thatcher would Know!)**, Book 022, much less: **"The Gospel According to our Elected King!" (The Good News from the Most Modern Perspective!)**, Book 077, which contains a very Special Sermon from Jesus Christ, himself!

07-52 [_] Yes, the Prayer of Faith will Save him from his Sickness, and the Supreme Ruler will Raise him Up in Good Health, when he Learns and Obeys the Dietary Laws of God; and, if he has Committed any Sins, they shall be Forgiven him. Yes, Confess your Faults to one another, and Pray for one another: so that you might be Healed. Remember this: the Effectual Fervent Prayer of a Righteous Man Avails much with God, who is even Willing to Raise Up Dead People. So, how much more Willing is he to Heal Sick People, who should Stop Drinking Bad Water, and Drink Pure Fresh Raw Fruit Juices, only — such as Watermelon Juice, which you can Squeeze Out through a Clean Cloth into a Bowl, and then set the Bowl in a larger Bowl of Ice, until it is Cold, which is one of the Best Drinks for Hardworking People during Hot Days, which will Cool them off, while also Nourishing their Bodies.

07-53 [_] Elijah was a Man of Great Faith, who was Subjected to Passions of Various Kinds, even as we are; and yet he Prayed Earnestly that it might not Rain on the Land of Israel; and it did not Rain on the whole Earth for the Space of 3 Years and 6 Months: because God saw that it was Necessary for Causing all such People to Repent of their Evils, which Saved their Souls, in spite of the Fact that many of them Died, who were then Recycled into New Bodies. After all, how else could all such People get to See all of the World within 6,000 Years? And then Elijah Prayed again, and the Sky gave Rain, and the Earth brought forth her Sweet Fruits, Nuts, Grasses, Grains, and all such Good Things.

07-54 [_] Now, you might Wonder if such a Great Drought did not make many Animals Extinct? Well, it likely did. However, the same Prayer of Faith can also Cause New Animals to be Raised Up, if they are Needed; and God Knows which ones are Needed for making the Earth into a Wonderful Paradise for everyone, which he is Happy to Raise Up for that Good Purpose; but, only IF his People are Living Righteous Lives, whereby they are Worthy of it. Meanwhile, Satan also has his Interests in Tormenting everyone as much as Possible. Therefore, he has Countless Pests, such as Mosquitoes, Ticks, Fleas, Bedbugs, Fire Ants, Hornets, Lice, Mice, Rats, Snakes and whatever else at his Disposal, which will one Glad Day be done away with, after People have Learned their Lessons.

07-55 [_] Brothers and Sisters, if any of you do go Astray from the Truth, and one Converts him; let him know that he who Converts the Sinner from the Errors of his own Evil Ways shall Save a Soul from Death, and shall Hid a Multitude of Sins.

— Chapter 08 —

Please Forward to John McArdle

08-01 [_] The Following Inspired Letter was sent to John McArdle at C-SPAN TV Network, who often Hosts the *Washington Journal*.

08-02 [_] Our Beautiful Brother John — a True Man with an Honest Heart and a Good Head!

08-03 [_] Thank you ever so much for having Elizabeth Grossman on your program, today, whereby the Consciences of some People might be a bit Awakened concerning some of the Realities of Life in **"The Divided States of United Lies!"** Too bad that ALL Members of Congress do not have to Carefully Listen to 3 Hours of that Extended Program (even if Chained and Shackled to their Chairs), and then Address that Important Subject for the remainder of the Day in the Big White OUTHOUSE in the District of High-ranking Criminals — like next Monday, with Elizabeth and her Colleagues seated beside of the Real Speaker of the House, and not with some Adopted Immature Beardless Sissy; and then Shut OFF all TV Channels, except for C-SPANDEX, Worldwide: so that everyone in the World can get their Ears Filled with TRUTHS about the EVILS of Capitalism! {See www.Amazon.com for: **"The BIG White OUTHOUSE on the Not-so-Biblical Capitol DUNGHILL!" (The Chief Sins of the Divided States of United Lies!) By The Worldwide People's Revolution!®** Book 023.}

08-04 [_] Of course, it might Help them to Relate with those Provable Truths, if they were all Dying with Cancers and other Horrible Diseases, while lying in Hospital Beds with Severe PAINS in their Heads, which should Infect every CONgressperson who does not Agree with: **"The Nature of CAPITALISM!" (A List of the EVILS of CAPITALISM!) By The Worldwide People's Revolution!®** Book 038. (See www.Amazon.com for a FREE Description of that Honest Book.)

08-05 [_] Indeed, if the Lawmakers were Plagued with all such Diseases, they might have a Tendency to come to their Right Senses with *the Prodigal Son of Luke 15;* but, seeing that they are well-paid to Campaign for 11 Months of Time out of every Year, and not Attend to their Business of Governing, not much will Change with a Capital C. Trust me, it will be the same Sad Song Next Year, even as it was Last Year, and for 40 Years before that! After all, no one is in Charge of anything in Washington, much less the TV Networks. Well, actually, the Rich Edomite Bankers and Drug Manufacturers and Insurance Agencies are in Charge of all of the Industrial Military Congressional Bankers' Complex, if you know what I Mean: beCause they Control the Money Supply, which can be Proven in a Courtroom with Law and Order, if anyone except the Tax Slaves, Insurance Slaves, Interest / Usury Slaves, Drug Slaves, Sex Slaves and Work Slaves are Interested in all such Truths. {See the above Link for the New MAGNIFIED Version of the Prodigal Son, in: **"SWANGKEENOMIKS Rules the Roost!" (How all People can Prosper in a RIIT WAA, and STOP Polluting the Earth with Capitalist TRASH!)**, Book 039, plus: **"The Environmentalists' Paradise!" (HOW almost Everyone could be Living in a Beautiful Manmade Paradise!)** Book 035. Otherwise, see: **"The New MAGNIFIED Version of the GOOD NEWS According to Saint LUKE!"** Book 061.}

08-06 [_] However, it could be that you, alone, my Trustworthy Honest Friend, are the one and only Person in the District of Criminals, who is even Slightly Interested in True Justice for ALL Peoples, Worldwide. However, there are many CONgressmen who would naturally Disagree with that Statement, and say that they are Interested in "America's Prosperity," only: because the other People of the World do not Matter — "to Hell with those Poor Mexicans," they are saying under their Breaths, while looking Disdainfully at the Statue of Liberty, and Conveniently Forgetting the Inscription on the Placard at her Feet. Perhaps that is WHY Americans have to Suffer with so many Massive Problems: beCAUSE of having Bad Attitudes toward other People in this World of Woes, who would also like to Raise their Standards of Living, who are just as Human as any of us, and more Human than most of those Greedy Selfish CONgresspeople, huh?

08-07 [_] It is now Time to make some DRASTIC Changes, beginning with our Hateful Lifestyles, Corporate GREED, and IGNORANCE! It is Time for some True Education with a Capital T and E. Yes, our Selected King has Connections with Almighty God, who might Judge us to be Worthy of the Seven Last Great Plagues, if we do not all REPENT and Change our Ways of Thinking and Living!

08-08 [_] Sincerely, your Faithful Friend, the Agitator!

08-09 [_] PS — Please Forward this Letter to Elizabeth Grossman and your Colleagues at C-SPANDEX. Thank you in advance, John. Keep up the Good Work. We all Love you very much! God Bless the Good People at C-SPAN.

08-10 [_] PPS — I Received Zero Response. So, what does that tell you about C-SPAN? {See www.Amazon.com for: **"The Washington Journal is a FARCE!" (C-SPAN Managers are not very WISE!) By The Worldwide People's Revolution!® Book 006**. It is possible, and most likely, that John never Received the Epistle from me: because it is so easy to hit the Delete Button on the Keyboard, which is **"The Nature of CAPITALISM!"**}

{FOOTNOTE: The Space below is Reserved for any Future Responses.}

— Chapter 09 —

The Irreverent LOUDMOUTH Sloth-gut Windbag Hole-in-his-Head Delivers another LONG Boring Sarcastic Sermon! †§

09-01 [_] O Selected King of **The Worldwide People's Revolution!®**, after reading your so-called 'New MAGNIFIED Version of the Epistle of JAMES,' I am Fully Persuaded that you are Mentally SICK: beCause you have Twisted the *Scriptures* to Fit with your own Agenda, which is SATANIC: beCause God has no Interest in us Building any Swanky Hotels, Castles, nor Fortresses: beCause he does not Want us to Solve our own Problems. Indeed, he Wants ALL of the Power and Glory for himself: because he is a little Selfish about that, which is why he clearly told Moses that he is a JEALOUS God, who will not give his Glory to anyone else — including Thyself, your Highness! Therefore, you might as well Abandon the Idea: because no such Beautiful Planned City States will ever be Built. Indeed, if they were, the Master Plan of the Master Farmer would be Frustrated, and no one would be Interested in Flying Away to Mount Zion on the Wings of an Imaginary Eagle, which would have to be no less than the Size of Noah's Ark, just to Carry his True Church into the Wilderness, unto that Holy Place which has Supposedly been Prepared for them, which is Actually just an American Concentration Camp, and NOT any Swanky Palaces, as you have Vainly Imagined. Indeed, why in the World would God go to all of the Trouble to Build Great Palaces for such Hypocritical Sinners as YOU, who are still Using those Abominations called CARS, Buses, Pickups, Trucks, and Airplanes, which do not Stink in the Nostrils of God: because he was the Holy One who Created all such Fossil Fuels for us to BURN! Yes, he Commanded us to Subdue the Earth, and have Dominion Over it, which we Capitalists have done most Efficiently for 1% of the People, who are the Rich People, who Deserve a thousand Times more Wealth than the Poor People, who make up about 80% of the People in this World of Woes, while the Remaining 19% of the People are called Tax Slaves, who Cover the Nakedness of Mankind, who alone are Worthy to Escape from the Great Tribulation: because they have been Paying the Bills, while the Poor People have been Living like Bloodsucking Leeches, whereby one Leech is Sucking on the Blood of another Leech, whereby the Farmers are Covered with Bloodsucking Leeches — that is, the Little Farmers, who are not Subsidized by the Federal Government: beCause they are too Small to be Qualified, who make up about 90% of the Farmers, who make up about 2% of the General Population, who Depend on them to Produce their Foods, or else they would Starve to Death: beCause, only one Person in a thousand or less has any Idea HOW to Grow their own Foods in America, who are Thinking about Retiring, or just Quitting: because there is no Way that they can Compete with Goliath and Sons, Incorporated, who have HUGE Farms and HUGE Tractors that Pull 400 Plows behind them, which no Farmer with a Mule or 2 can Compete with, much less a Farmer with a Garden Tiller, who might Attend to 5 Acres; but, no more, while Burning Up all of their Income in that Tiller, which can Drink Up no less 20$ every Day when it is Used: beCause Gasoline-powered Tillers and Lawnmowers are very Inefficient Tools to Work with, when Compared with Electric Tools. †§‡

(HOW the True Church will Escape from the Great Tribulation!)

09-02 [_] For Example, an Electric Tiller might use all of 2$-worth of Electricity during an entire Day of Tilling, while that Gasoline-powered Tiller might use 40$-worth of Gas, while Stinking up the Air with Fragrant Capitalist Toxic Odors that Cause the Holy Angels to Rejoice each Night at the Barrooms that they Attend with Saint Peter and the Apostle Paul, who Smoke those Foot-long Cuban Cigars, and Drink Tequila and Vodka mixed with the Blood of Holy Muslims, who Worship Buzzeldick the Great, who is the Father of Allah, who was one of a hundred or so Arabian Gods, which you can Learn about in *Wickedpedia,* which still Holds Tightly to the Federal Government LIES about what Actually Happened during September 11th, 2001, whereby all Doubters in their False Reports are Classified and Demonized as "Conspiracy Theorists," along with whomever Doubts that Lee Harvey Oswald Assassinated President John Kennedy with a Single Silver Bullet, and then laid itself down on a Hospital Gurney in Dall-ass, Tex-ass, in Pristine Condition, after Blowing the Backside of his Head half Off from the REAR, from Behind him, which is what all Silver Bullets do when they are Shot by Communists. Indeed, anyone who has Studied Ballistics would Know that for a FACT: beCause it is just a Natural Thing that Happens when a Bullet goes Wild from the Pistol of some Lone CIA Ranger, after Entering into the Backside of some President's Head, whereby it Turns itself around, and Blasts Off a Quarter of his Skull, which can be Proven in any Courtroom with Law and Order — except that it would Cost too much to Experiment with the Corpse of an Executed Prisoner, who has been Executed for Murdering the Grandmother of Capitalism, if you knoweth what I meaneth. Well, actually, to be Perfectly Honest with thee, I do not know what I mean; but, it Sounded Good: beCause your Selected King Mocks Capitalism, as if it were a BAD Economic System, when God Knows for a Fact that it is the Economic Salvation of the World! †§‡§§

09-03 [_] Indeed, People were Extremely Poor, until Capitalism came along, and People began Buying Stocks and Bonds in Coke Companies, Cigar Companies, Cigarette Companies, Whiskey Companies, Car Companies, and so on; and then we FLOURISHED! Yes, the American Dream became a Reality for Rich Red Jew Bankers, O Selected King, who Loaned Money to millions of Poor Would-be Capitalists, who got themselves into Millions of Failing Capitalist Businesses with that Borrowed Money, and ended up Paying those Rich Edomite Bankers TRILLIONS of Dollars in Interest Payments: beCause they were and still are most Worthy among Men, being the Elite Class with Pinocchio Noses a Mile Long: beCause, like almost all Red Jews, they like to Exaggerate Things: beCause it is Second Nature to them, even as Deceit is Second Nature to someone who Packs Fruits in a Box, who just Naturally puts the Bad Fruits in the Bottom of the Box, and Covers them up with some Good Fruits: beCause Capitalism Forces them to CHEAT. Yes, they must get Money somehow, just to Pay all of those Hateful Taxes, Insurance Bills, Health Care nonsense, and Constant Repairs: beCause almost everything is Designed for the Trash Dump! Yes, the Cars are Engineered to start having Problems within a 2 or 3 Years: so that a Person is Forced to get them Repaired, or to Buy 3 New Cars, and let some Poor Capitalist Pay for the Repairs, who does not Realize what a TRAP it is, whereby all of those Capitalists are Forever in DEBT to those Friendly Banksters, and Especially if a Person should get Sick from Eating some Capitalist Garbage, which is Filled with Holy Chemicals, Preservatives, and Yellow Dye Number 5, which gives to them Sexy Red Lips, even without Lipstick, while also giving to them Liver Problems: beCause the Liver has no Idea what to Do with 500+ Harmful Chemicals during just one Day. †§‡§§

09-04 [_] For Example, there are 60 to 80 Different Added Chemicals in the Process of making Fine Beers — such as Budstupido and Miller Low-life; but, not to Worry: because you can always

Drink Expensive Imported all-Natural Beers from Germany, which follows the 1678 Pure Beer Code, which Requires all-Natural Ingredients in the Industrial Water that runs through Hamburg, which is still a little Holier than the Recycled Sewage Water below Saint Louis, Mizeree, which is the Home of Budstupido. Yes, you can even find Pure Colorado Mountain Spring Water, which has been Flowing down from Abandoned Gold Mines, which Water is Laden with Mercury, Lead, Arsenic, Cadmium, and other Holy Ingredients of Capitalism, which you could also Unwittingly Use to Water your own LUSCIOUS All-Mineral Organic Garden, while Sincerely Believing that all such Foods are GOOD to Eat: because they are "Home-grown"! Yes, the Acid Rains also Sprinkle your Fruits and Vegetables with Holy Water, whereby you are Blest with Chemtrails in the Clear Blue Skies, which are more of those "Conspiracy Theories," according to *Wickedpedia*: because your Loving Anti-Christ Federal Sinless Cover-up Government would never do anything to Offend the Baby Jesuses of the World: beCause SINator Blabbermouth LOVES them. Indeed, he is not even Aware that his Generous Government has Sprayed no less than 200 Billion Tons of Chemical Dung in the Atmosphere, including Millions of Tons of Aluminum, which has Poisoned the Land, Rivers, Lakes, Mountains, Fruit Trees, Vegetable Gardens, Grasslands, Forests, and everything below those Jet Airplanes, which are the Holiest of all Capitalist Inventions: beCause they make it Possible for TV Stars to Eat Breakfast in New Yuck City, Lunch in Miami, and Supper in Lost Angels, Californicate, and then go to Rome for Romance during the Weekend: beCause Capitalism makes that Possible, which even Jesus Christ would Approve of: beCause he Hated Poverty, which is WHY he Taught the Truth about a RIGHTEOUS One-World Government; but, those Red Jews, who Controlled the Translations and Publishing of all Bibles, made Sure that all such Information was Edited OUT: beCause it was a Great Threat to their EVIL Capitalist Empire, which Depends on IGNORANCE! †§‡§§

09-05 [_] Yes, Ignorance among the Masses of People, Worldwide, is the Primary Objective of Capitalist Pigs: beCause it would not be very Profitable for them, if the Masses of People should Learn that it is Possible and most Practical for everyone to Live within **"GLORIOUS Swanky Hotels Castles and Fortresses!" (Beautiful Planned City States for WISE Intelligent Well-Educated People with Common Sense and Good Understanding!)**, Book 019: because of having more than 5,000 Advantages over normal Cities of Confusion, which are Designed for Eternal Debts, Unemployment, Hunger, Riots, Strikes, Police Brutalities, Election Deceptions, and even Civil Wars: beCause of POVERTY! Indeed, when was the last Time that you saw 2 Rich Men having a Fight over the Garbage in a Dumpster? Indeed, only Extremely Poor People would do such Things, which is most often done in Capitalist Countries: because they cannot Afford **"The LUSCIOUS All-Mineral Organic Method of Gardening!" (HOW to Grow DELICIOUS Satisfying Foods for Potential Kingz and Kweenz in Swanky PALACES!)**, Book 021: beCause, "it costs too much." Yes, it is similar to Capitalist Wages, which are Preferably Minimum Wages: beCause, if some Work Slave should Earn 50$ per Hour for Hoeing Weeds in a Garden, those Cheap Potatoes might Cost 1$ per Pound, even though a Person can Dig Up no less than 2,400 Pounds of them per Day, taking his sweet Time! In Fact, I have Personally Dug Up no less than 2,000 Pounds during just 4 Hours! Therefore, with Mechanical Slaves to do 90% or more of the Work for us, those Potatoes should be 10 Cents per Pound — except that those Tractors Cost a half million dollars! Therefore, they must be Paid for by Mass Production. †§‡§§

09-06 [_] Now, you might be Wondering just Exactly what all of that Nonsense has to do with Escaping to Mount Zion, in order to Avoid the Great Tribulation? Well, if you Lived on the Land, and were Well Set Up for Living on the Land, like almost all People could be and should be:

(HOW the True Church will Escape from the Great Tribulation!)

beCause of your Righteous Government Assisting you to get Set Up Properly, you would not be Suffering through any "Great Tribulation": beCause there would be no such a Thing! However, there is a certain Diabolical Religion that Teaches another BIG LIE — that God Wants us to SUFFER, in Order to Perfect our Souls, which Doctrine is Supported by the *Holy Bible,* which Explains WHY there are NO Reasonable Solutions for anything within that Unholy Mutilated Bible! — well, except for PRAYING. Yes, we are Invited to Pray — as if Noah could have been Saved from the Great Flood, if he had only PRAYED! Actually, the Bible does Suggest that we Love our Naaberz az much az we Love ourselves, whereby it might cross our Weak Minds that only the Amish and Mennonites DO that when they Build Houses and Barns, whereby they Sacrifice any Personal Gain for the Welfare and Benefit of all of them: beCause they Realize that they will all be much Richer, if they are all Moderately Rich at Young Ages. Therefore, the whole Community Contributes a Day or 2 of Work, in order to get a New Family "on their Feet," whereby that Family can be Debt-free, and have a Chance to Win in the Capitalist Game. However, they did not Learn that "Bad Habit" from Capitalists; but, it was Handed Down to them by their Traditions, which were Learned at a Time when it was a Matter of Survival. Indeed, the Pioneers in America also had that same Good Attitude when they were Building their Log Cabins: beCause it is about a hundred Times easier to Build such a Cabin with the Assistance of 10 Strong Men, or at least with the Help of some Workhorses, who can Roll the Heavy Logs into Place by Means of Log Ramps, Ropes and Pulleys, even if those Logs are 2 feet in Diameter and 40 feet Long. †§‡

09-07 [_] However, in the Capitalist System, you are Lucky to Find even one True Friend: because most of the People are made into Greedy Selfish little PIGS, who only Think of their own Gain, and by whatever Means WORKS — even if they have to Steal, Lie, Swindle, Rob, or whatever is Convenient at the Time: beCause most Capitalists HATE to do Physical Work — such as Mixing up Concrete. However, if they can get someone to do it for them at Minimum Wages, that is Okay, just as long as they are getting 10 to 100 Times as much Money for their Work. Indeed, many Chief Executives get 400 to 1,000 Times as much Money, and they still Want more, in Order to Fulfill their All-American Dreams, and: "To Hell with anyone else!" Personally, I find it Difficult to Believe that any such People will have any Positions in the Kingdom of the Gods; but, most of them Imagine themselves to be very Important People, and probably the First to Enter into that Holy Kingdom: beCause they have given Money for Cancer Research, or otherwise they have Donated something to the Food Bank, which not even the Hogs Want to Eat, let alone the Hungry Children, who are Starving for Good Wholesome Natural Foods, which are Grown in a LUSCIOUS All-Mineral Organic Garden. †§‡ {NOTE: You can see many Photos with Explanations in: **"Orgimmick Gardening at its Best!" (HOW to Grow Delicious Satisfying Foods without a 10-Million-Dollar Investment!) By The Worldwide People's Revolution!® Book 079.**}

09-08 [_] So, O Selected King, the Great Question is this: "Will Evil People like you have any Positions in the Government of God?" Most likely not: because you have only Served yourself, and have never done any Good Thing for Mankind, which can be Proven in a Courtroom. †§‡§§

09-09 [_] Well, O Irreverent LOUDMOUTH Sloth-gut Windbag Hole-in-Thy-Head, your Speech would be an Abomination, if it were not for all of the Great Truths that Slip Out of your Head, whereby you Prove yourself to be WRong, over and over. Yes, your Arguments are rather Weak, and Ineffective to Change any Minds. †§‡ {See: **"All of the Arguments are in Favor of our Selected King, who has Zero Challengers!" (Before you Attend another Election Deception,**

you should Carefully Study this Inspired Book with an Honest Open Mind!) By The Worldwide People's Revolution!® Book 085.}

09-10 [_] O Selected King, I do Wish you and yours all of the Good Luck in the World: because you will Need it, if you are going to Escape from the Power and Control of the BEAST that now Rules Over you. Indeed, they have Spy Satellites in the Sky, Drones to Snoop around with, even as small as Honeybees, as well as Wiretapping, Computer Eavesdropping, and more than you can Imagine for Spying on you and whomever might Plan on Escaping. Besides that, every Airplane Trip must be Reported to the Aeronautics Control Center, just to get Off of the Ground; or else such Airplanes will be Shot Down — that is, unless those Planes are Flown during September 11th, 2001, in which Case they can get by with Murder. (See www.AE911TRUTH.org for the Proof.) †§‡§§

09-11 [_] Well, those Foxes can be Outfoxed by Extra Intelligent People, if they know what to Do, which Requires more Innovation than Education, even though Education and Practical Experiences are very Important for Success. After all, an Airplane that is large enough to Carry 10,000 or more People at one Time, would have to be rather LARGE, and would have to have Special Runways, just to Take Off and Land it. Nevertheless, where there is a Will, there is a Way. †§‡

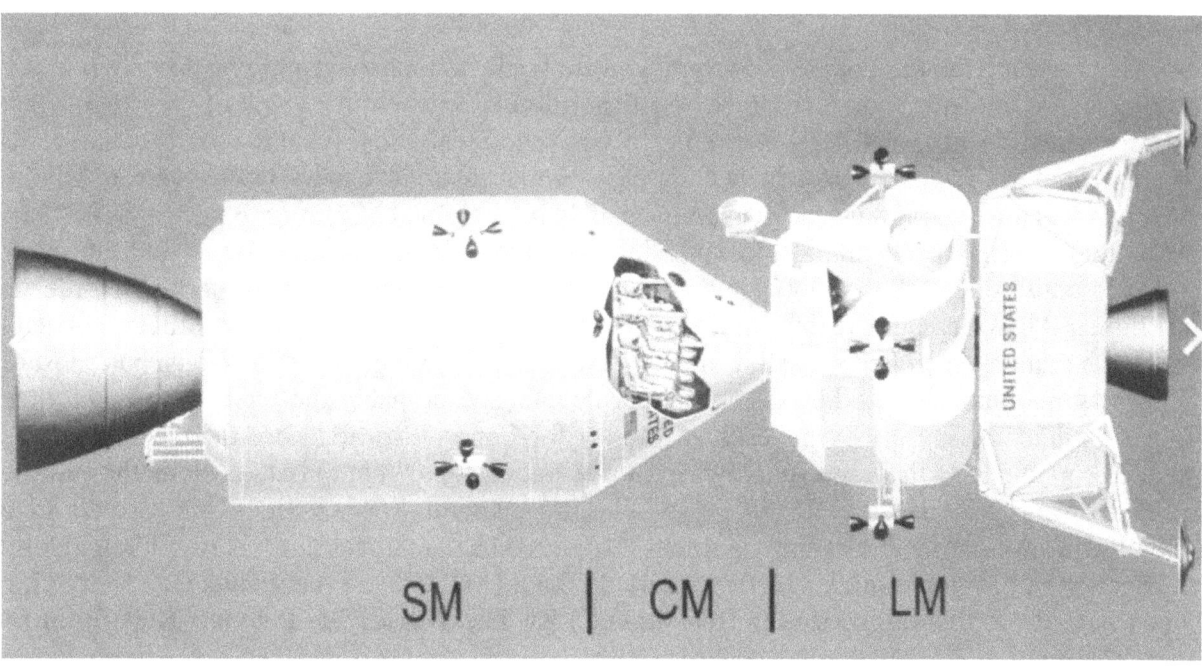

{FOOTNOTE: The Lunar Landing Module is to the far Right. Where is the Rocket Launcher for it on the Moon? Where is the Minimum 100,000-gallon Fuel Tank for it to Blast Off at 4,000 MpH? See *Wickedpedia* for all of the Details that Explain just HOW the NASA Magicians did it!}

09-12 [_] O Selected King, being an Architect and an Engineer, you should know the Impracticality of making any such Airplane, which would be too Big and too Heavy to even get itself Off of the Ground: beCause, when such a Ship is made very Large, it must also be made very Strong, which Means that it must be Strengthened by Heavier Stronger Steel, or Aluminum Trusses, which can only be just so Large, and then the WEIGHT of the Airplane is Working

Against itself, and especially when it is Loaded Down with 10,000+ People! Therefore, it is less Practical than going to the Moon, which Required no less than 900,000 Gallons of Rocket Fuel to get there, and only 100 Gallons to Return, if you can Believe it! Personally, I do NOT Believe it: beCause it is Physically Impossible. However, I Suggest that you Build a HUGE Blimp, which would have to be no less than 2 Miles Long and a half-mile Wide and High, whereby a Strong Wind could CRASH IT into a Mountain! †§‡§§

09-13 [_] O Selected King, it is Obvious that no such a "Great Eagle" can be Workable. Besides that, a Blimp, like the Zeppelins, would never Work: beCause the Hole in the North is not Big Enough to Accommodate it. Indeed, it is only a hundred Miles in Diameter. †§‡§§

09-14 [_] Well, I have no Idea just how BIG the Hole is, nor how big the Airplane would have to be: because it could be that less than 1,000 People might Qualify to Escape from the Great Tribulation, which would NOT Include myself: beCause I am NOT a Holy Man — at least not yet. However, we never know what a Day might bring forth, nor WHO will get Inspired to Help us to Escape. After all, if all of these Things are Preordained by God to Happen, then they Will Happen by one Means or another. Therefore, I am not going to Worry myself over it for even a Minute: beCause I have Faith in God to Provide whatever is Needed for the True Church to Escape.

09-15 [_] O Selected King, if you are not Personally going to Escape, WHY do you Care about anyone else Escaping?

09-16 [_] Well, it is my Love for Innocent Souls that makes that Possible. Therefore, I will Gladly Do whatever I can Do to make it Possible, and Especially if I am the Elected King of the New RIGHTEOUS One-World GovernMINT! Yes, I will then be in a Position whereby I might be of more Assistance, whereby it will become Possible. {See www.Amazon.com for: **"Mark Twain Races for the PRESIDENCY!" (The 2020 Presidential Candidates Desperately Need Some STRONG Undefeatable COMPETITION!)**, Book 033, plus: **"The Gospel According to our Elected King!" (The Good News from the Most Modern Perspective!) By The Worldwide People's Revolution!® Book 077.**}

09-17 [_] O Selected King, why is it that almost everything in the *Bible* is written in Mysterious Ways, so that few People can Understand it — such as the Information in *the Book of Revelation* about the Woman / Church Flying Away on the Wings of a Great Eagle? Is that not Obvious NONSENSE — as in Edomite Mythology?

09-18 [_] Well, to be frankly Honest with you, I would say that it is Pure Nonsense, unless you have the Capacity to Imagine that a "Great Eagle" is a Great Airplane of some Kind. Remember that some of those Biblical "Eagles" had 6 Wings. Therefore, that Special "Eagle" might have 60 Wings and 120 Jet Engines, for all that I would know. Yes, it could be that it will be able to Lift itself Up like a Helicopter, and then Fly like an Airplane on its Wings, and then Land like an Eagle, or like a Helicopter might Land. Moreover, it could be Powered by Rechargeable Batteries, which could be Recharged by Manpower by Means of Bicycle Pedals within the Airplane, which would make the Power Source quite Reliable, which could be Supplemented by Solar Power, and also by Wind Power, once the Plane is Flying: because of having Turbines with Vanes on Top of the Wings, which Drive the Propellers of the Airplane. In other Words, it would be a rather Complicated Machine, to say the least about it; but, if it Works, that is Good enough. After all, it would be a one-time Trip to make.

09-19 [_] O Selected King, would such a Complicated Machine not have to be TESTED, before 10,000+ People might be KILLED by it?

09-20 [_] Well, it is a Scientific FACT that the Lunar Landing Module (LEM) was NOT Tested before it Landed on the Moon, and Safely Returned to the Command Module at 4,000 Miles per Hour (MpH). Therefore, such a Spaceship, called the *Eagle,* in *the Book of Revelation,* should be able to Travel at 200 MpH with no Adverse Effects. Moreover, it would be Testable before being Deployed, while the Apollo 11 Moon Mission *Eagle* was NOT Testable! Indeed, it was a one-time Shot with Good Luck, you might say, and it Worked Flawlessly on the First Landing, and for several Times after that: beCause NASA knew Exactly what to Expect on the Moon, and how to Compensate for any Miscalculations, Guaranteed. Therefore, if they could get that Lunar Module to BLAST OFF at 4,000 MpH with only 5 Gallons of Rocket Fuel, I reckon that we could get an Airplane going 200 MpH with Helicopter Propellers that also Work as Vanes for Electric Turbines, after the Airplane is Slowly but Surely Flying North. Indeed, those same Propellers can be used to Motivate the Airplane in any Direction, which will be Assisted by the Wind, itself, as well as by the Sunlight on Top of those 60 Wings, which will have Solar Collectors, as well as by the Pedal-powered Turbines within the Airplane, itself, whereby X-amount of Healthy Young Men can take Turns Recharging the Batteries for each Propeller on the Wings: because each one should be Independent from the others, for the Purpose of Total Electronic Control, whereby it Guides itself, even as certain Cars can now Drive themselves. Therefore, if there are some Backup Batteries for Emergencies, everything should Work quite Well. After all, if it is Necessary, such an Airplane can be Landed in almost any Field, until the Batteries are Recharged again — that is, if those Young Men are getting too Tired from Pedaling, and need to Rest for a Day or 2, whereby they can Recharge their own Batteries, you might say. †

— Chapter 10 —

Can the Eagle not be Hydrogen-powered?

10-01 [_] Well, to Fly all of the Way from Texas into the Hollow Earth, it would Require Refueling 2 or 3 Times, just to get in there: beCause we are talking about thousands of Miles for a HUGE Airplane, being Fully Loaded with People, Water, Fruit Juices, Foods, Clothing, Tools, Repair Parts, and Personal Belongings. Therefore, to Power such a Ship with Hydrogen would be Impractical: because it would Require an Equal Amount of Space to Store the Hydrogen, itself, for such a Long Journey. Besides that, those Young Men need something to Do, just to keep them Busy, and to make them Feel Good about themselves when they Arrive at their Destination, which is Unknown, which might Require another Week to get there. Whatever the Case, if the Great Eagle can be Powered by Men, alone, then it is Reliable: because, if no such a Holy City is not Discovered within a Week or so, then they can keep Searching for it, until they Run Out of Water and Foods, in which Case they would be Forced to Land and Search for Water and Foods, which could Prove to be Interesting within the Hollow Earth. Indeed, the Foods would most likely be very Strange to us, and might even make us Sick.

(HOW the True Church will Escape from the Great Tribulation!)

10-02 [_] O Selected King, did you not say that you are Unworthy to Escape from the Great Tribulation? So, why are you writing as if you will be Onboard the Great Eagle?

10-03 [_] Well, even if I am Unworthy to Escape, it does not Mean that I will not go along with them: beCause, who else is Able to Communicate with God, just in Case they get into Trouble?

10-04 [_] O Selected King, if you could Communicate with God, you would already Know Exactly where Mount Zion is Located, and Exactly how many People will be going there, and Exactly what is Required for getting there, Safely. †§‡

10-05 [_] Well, God does not Do for us whatever we are Able to Do for ourselves: beCause it is a Test of our Faith, Hope, Trust, Love, Patience, Persistence, and Obedience, whereby we can be Saved by the Skins of our Teeths, you might say, just the same as Lot and his 2 Daughters Escaped from Sodom. Indeed, with that Plan, no one can Brag about Saving themselves: beCause it is only by the Grace of God that anyone will be Saved, even as it always is: beCause that is the Nature of Things in this Crazy World. Yes, you can also Read about that in Chapter 12 of *Revelation,* which Church just Barely Escapes by the Skin of her Teeth! — not that our Teeths have any Skins; but, that it is a Good Comparison, or Figure of Speech.

10-06 [_] O Selected King, I would say that you would be spending your time much more wisely, if you used it to write **"The New MAGNIFIED Version of The Book of MORMON!" (The Story of the White and Dark Indians in the Americas!) By The Worldwide People's Revolution!®** Book 040. After all, it might have some Spiritual Value, while this Nonsense is of no Value to anyone: beCause there is no Mount Zion within the Hollow Earth: beCause there is no Hollow Earth. Indeed, if there were, NASA would have already Discovered it, and Reported the Truth about it, just like they Reported the Truth about UFO's, saying that no such Things Exist! However, there have been more than a MILLION Sightings of them by hundreds of thousands of People, including yourself, O Selected King. Therefore, NASA can be Trusted. †§‡§§

10-07 [_] Well, I would say that the Least Trusted Government in the World is that of **"The Divided States of United Lies!" (The so-called "United States of North America" in Disguise!)**, Book 058, which most Definitely does not Want most People to Learn that the Inside of the Earth is Inhabited by BILLIONS of People: beCause there is at least 4 Times as much Land on the Inside as on the Outside! Indeed, there are no Oceans on the Inside, which is a Paradise with its own Central Sun, as I have said before, which is NOT a Bright Light, like our Sunstar; but, it is Sufficient to make the Trees and all other Plants Grow Well. In Fact, it is the Home of many Kinds of Aliens, who Think of us as the Barbarians: beCause we are Murderous Barbarians! How can anyone Rightly Deny it? Just Listen to the *Washington Journal,* if you Doubt it. †§‡

10-08 [_] O Selected King, if what you say is True, how come those Aliens do not just Appear to us in broad open Daylight, in the New York City Central Park, for Example?

10-09 [_] Well, they likely Realize that Redneck Zealots would Murder them for the "Fun of it." After all, Americans have more than 300,000,000 Personal Weapons to Fire at them. Therefore, it is Safer to just stay away from us. Besides that, Americans have been Terribly Spooked by Horror Movies, whereby their Imaginations can go Wild in the Presence of Aliens.

10-10 [_] So, O Selected King, what about Atomic Power for Escaping on the Wings of that Great Eagle? Would that not be the most Practical Way to Obtain Unlimited Power in all Airplanes? Moreover, when one of them Crashes, the nearby People could Obtain some Radioactive Flavoring in their Bones, whereby they might Obtain more Cancers, which would give those Medical Doctors something to Do, to keep them Busy in their Laboratories for Cancer Research, which would Improve on the Great False Economy. †§‡§§

— Chapter 11 —

WHO will Qualify to Escape?

11-01 [_] According to most Modern Churches, almost everyone is "going to heaven when they die," according to the Irreverent Snake, who Wears a Multicolored Coat of Self-deceptions and Colorful Lies: beCause he Knows for a Fact that HE is NOT going to Heaven when he Dies, and neither is anyone else: beCause this Earth is our Eternal Home — that is, unless we are found Unworthy to Live here, in which Case we will be Cast Down to a Lower Order of Worlds, which is 7 Times Worse than here! (See *Deuteronomy 28 and Leviticus 26* for the Proof.) ‡

11-02 [_] O Selected King, what about *John 3:13,* which clearly states: *"No Man has Ascended up to Heaven, except for the Son of a Man of Holiness, who came down from Heaven, who is now in an Heavenly Condition, while you, O Nicodemus, are in a Hellish Condition, and do not even Realize it: because your Spiritual Eyes are Blinded, and your Spiritual Ears are Deafened, so that you cannot even Hear the Truth of it."* — NMV

11-03 [_] Well, that seems to Agree with what I was saying — that no Man goes to Heaven when he Dies, even if he is a Holy Man like Moses, whose Face Shined with the Glory of God: beCause this Earth is our Eternal Home, which is WHY the Lord's Prayer reads: *"Your Kingdom Come, and your Will be Done on the Earth, even as it is now Done in Heavenly Places, O God."* Yes, someone may Deny that *that* is the Correct Interpretation of it. However, there are many *Scriptures* that Support that Doctrine, which can be Proven to be True in a Courtroom, whether or not anyone Likes it. Indeed, most People Want to Escape from this World, and as soon as Possible; but, behold, they will be the Last to Enter into the Kingdom of God: beCause they should have been making this World a much Better Place to Live, rather than Help to make it into such a Hellish Place to Live, whereby they Want to Escape from it, and mostly from their own Self-inflicted Torments. Indeed, if you had to Pack a 200-pound Bag of Beans on your Back, all Day long, every Day, you too would likely Want to get RID of it, even if you had to Kill yourself, which many People do: beCause they Want to Escape from their own Self-inflicted Torments. However, the Right Way to Escape from all such Torments is to FAST and PRAY, until you Realize what is most Needed, which is Fresh Clean Air, Pure Living Water, Wholesome Natural Foods, Natural Clothing, Secure Houses, Luscious All-Mineral Organic Gardens, Cisterns full of Clean Water, Home-craft Workshops, Well-made Tools, and Beautiful Self-air-conditioned Stone Dome Homes within Beautiful Tax-free Insurance-free Interest-free Planned City States, whereby all People can Prosper and Live in Peace on the Earth, which can be made into a Paradise for everyone! {See www.Amazon.com for: **"The Environmentalists' Paradise!"** (HOW almost Everyone could

be Living in a Beautiful Manmade Paradise!) By The Worldwide People's Revolution!® Book 035.}

11-04 [_] O Selected King, HOW could we SEPARATE the Good People from the Bad People, without Producing more Bad People? After all, it is/are the Good Peoples who Help to make other Bad Peoples into Good Peoples: because Goodness is Stronger than Evilness, which is why most Peoples in the World are Christians, Muslims, Hindus, Buddhists, or something Religious.

11-05 [_] Well, they will just Naturally Separate themselves when they Check the Appropriate Boxes in: **"The Complete SURVEYS of our VALUES!"** Book 059. Yes, that Good Book contains many SURVEYS of our VALUES, whereby the Good Peoples can easily be Discovered, who can Join Up with Like-minded Peoples, and then Build their own **"GLORIOUS Swanky Hotels Castles and Fortresses!" (Beautiful Planned City States for WISE Intelligent Well-Educated People with Common Sense and Good Understanding!)**, Book 019, whereby they will be Free from Tax Slavery, Interest Slavery, Insurance Slavery, Drug Slavery, Sex Slavery, and Work Slavery: beCause True Christians are FREE in all Ways. Otherwise, they have the WRong Doctrines Stuck in their Heads, which must be Removed by the Sword of Truths.

11-06 [_] So, O Selected King, if a Person is Perfectly Honest: beCause of being HUMBLE, such a Person might Escape from the Great Tribulation, huh?

11-07 [_] Well, such a Person would have to be Honest about all Subjects, including the Provable Truths about those Stinking Noisy Cars, Vans, Pickups, Trucks, Buses, Tractors, Bulldozers, Lawnmowers, Weed-eaters, Chainsaws, Garden Tillers, Motorcycles, Motor Scooters, Motorboats, Snowmobiles, Snow Blowers, Leaf Blowers, and all other Gasoline-powered Tools, including those most Abominable Airplanes! {See www.Amazon.com for: **"The Nature of CAPITALISM!" (A List of the EVILS of CAPITALISM!)**, Book 038, plus: **"SWANGKEENOMIKS Rules the Roost!" (HOW all People can Prosper in a RIIT WAA, and STOP Polluting the Earth with Capitalist TRASH!) By The Worldwide People's Revolution!®** Book 038.}

11-08 [_] O Selected King, are there no CARS in Mount Zion? How in the World do they get to Work over there without Cars?

11-09 [_] Well, have you ever Heard of Elevators and Electric Subway Trains? Indeed, they have something similar; but, much Better: beCause their Trains are Quiet, Comfortable, Spacious, Clean, and Toll-Free. However, most of the People simply get up and go to Work at Home, or near Home: beCause it is most Practical for each Person to Grow his own Foods, and make his own Clothing from Cloth that has been Produced by Machines: because there is a Time and Place for all such Things; but, no one is a Tax Slave of any Kind, much less a Usury Slave, Insurance Slave, Drug Slave, nor Sex Slave: because a Good Economy does not have any of those Evil Things, even as I have Proven in the above mentioned Books.

11-10 [_] So, O Selected King, it Sounds like most of us will be left Behind, huh? Indeed, we are not Willing to Live without our Capitalist Abominations; and therefore, we will not Qualify to Enter into that Holy City, where no Painted Skunks nor Poisonous Snakes are Allowed.

— Chapter 12 —

Comforting Words for those People who are Left Behind

12-01 [_] O Selected King, if we are Left Behind, we will have to go through the Great Tribulation, which will be no Fun at all, huh?

12-02 [_] Well, you can make it a lot more Fun, just by Cooperating with me: beCause, if most People DO what I say, it will be a Wonderful Time to Live. However, Strangely enough, most People will NOT Do what I Teach; and therefore, they will have to Suffer with the Tyranny of some Anti-Christ DICTATOR, who will be much Worse than Adolf Hitler: beCause every Move will be Watched by that Bad Government, whereby your Freedoms will simply Disappear; and almost everyone will become Depressed by it all, while Regretting that they did not Love nor OBEY my Inspired Words of Provable Truths. After all, if everyone did Love and Obey my Teachings, almost everyone would end up Living in those **"Beautiful Swanky PALACES!" (A New Concept in Living Habits — Swanky Palaces for Poor People!) By The Worldwide People's Revolution!®**, Book 066.

12-03 [_] So, O Selected King, it Sounds as if we will get just Exactly what we Deserve for Rejecting your Inspired Words of Provable Truths, huh?

12-04 [_] Well, I must Confess that you are Right: beCause it was Certainly NOT my Choice to Continue to Live in this Capitalist HELL, which Produces a Handful of Extremely Rich People, while Producing Multitudes of Extremely Poor SLAVES. Indeed, I have said and written whatever is Needed for True Prosperity; but, it seems that almost no one is Interested in it: beCause of Maintaining their "American Dreams," which are rather Selfish, Greedy, and Insane! After all, not one Person in a MILLION ever Obtains a Good Dream, whereby they have Fresh Clean Air to Breathe, Pure Living Water to Drink, Wholesome Natural Foods to Eat, and Secure Houses to Live in, much less be Able to Live in Peace without any Fears: beCause there is always the Possibility of Atomic Bombs falling on them for the Lack of **"The New RIGHTEOUS One-World Government!" (HOW to Establish a RIGHTEOUS One-World Government without Going to WAR!) By The Worldwide People's Revolution!®** Book 056.

12-05 [_] O Selected King, the Communist Chinese finally got themselves on the Capitalist Bandwagon, and went "Whole Hog" for what they Imagined would be True Prosperity, and even Built several Vacant Cities, which they Hoped would be Occupied by American-style Capitalists; but, behold, the Idea Backfired, and almost everyone in China LOST. Nevertheless, they have Managed to Build more Interstate Highways than us Americans, and are also Polluting their Air with Capitalist Abominations — such as those Electric Power Plants, which are Powered by COAL, which is so Polluting that one cannot See Clearly for one City Block in Beijing, during most Days. However, when the Sky is "Clear," one can see for about 2 City Blocks. Therefore, if the Chinese had any Sense, they would Immediately Confess the Errors of their Ways, and get themselves to Work on those **"GLORIOUS Swanky Hotels Castles and Fortresses,"** which are Designed for Eternal Employment. However, with so much Pollution from those ElecTrickery Power Plants, it is Doubtful that any of the Fruit Trees would Survive anywhere around Beijing. †§‡

12-06 [_] Well, they should have Consulted with me before they took up the Song of the American Drunkards. However, they Obviously did not know that I Existed, and still have no Great Interest in my Ideas: beCause they are Naturally very Proud of their own Great "Successes," which are quite Impressive, when Compared with some of their Poor Naaberz; but, with such BAD Air to Breathe, and such PUTRID Water to Drink, and such Insipid Fruits and Vegetables to Eat, one can Honestly say that they have a very LOW Standard of Living, even when Compared with India, which at least has enough Poverty to Minimize the Cars on the Highways, when Compared with Chinese Capitalist Highways, which are like Lost Angels, Californicate, almost every Day, except that one can Hardly Breathe in Beijing. Therefore, the People are using their own Lungs as Air Filters, and their Bodies as Garbage Disposal Dumps, while Imagining that Life is Pretty Good for them, when it is Obvious that it was much Better when most of them Lived on the Land, and knew nothing about Capitalism, which has Proven itself to be the Death of them! ‡

12-07 [_] So, O Selected King, is there any Way to Un-inspire them, now that they have been Tainted with Capitalist LIES? Are they not Redeemable, at all?

12-08 [_] Well, do you Think that Americans are Redeemable, at all? Indeed, some of them no doubt are; but, the Vast Majority of them have their Heads Stuck up the Rectum of Uncle Sam, and could never Pull them Out: beCause they have been "Sold Down the River with Poor Nigger Jim," if you know what I Mean. Yes, they are Victims of Capitalism, which Binds them with very Deceptive Chains, which are Conveniently called: "Freedom," "Liberty," "Democracy," and "Justice for all," even though they are nothing but Education Slaves, Work Slaves, Tax Slaves, Interest Slaves, Insurance Slaves, Drug Slaves, Sex Slaves, and Endless Bills Slaves for the most Part. Nevertheless, they do have Freedom to Run their Mouths, just like I have Freedom to Write about it; but, of what Value is it, if almost no one Pays any Attention? Yes, you can Hear their Complaints on the *Washington Journal,* on the C-SPANDEX TV Network, which is Commercial-free, which Permits People to Call in with their Questions and Complaints, which I have written about in: **"The Washington Journal is a FARCE!" (C-SPAN Managers are not very WISE!)**, Book 006, which is quite Educational, and Humorous.

12-09 [_] O Selected King, why do you not Waste some Money and Time, and Call them with your OWN Honest Opinions?

12-10 [_] Well, the *Washington Journal* Format is not Suited to the Honest Opinions of People who can Think and Remember, who are not given Enough Time to Express such Opinions in such a Way as to Persuade anyone to Believe the Truth. Indeed, not even a Whole Book contains Enough Words to Persuade most People to Believe any given Subject. For Example, how many People now Believe that the Earth is Hollow with the Limited Amount of Information within this Inspired Book, which is not Designed to Persuade them to Believe any such Things, even as the *Bible* is also not Designed to do that; but, it does Mention it in one Verse, which I have Quoted in a Previous Chapter, which I am Sure did not Persuade anyone to Believe it: beCause most People just Naturally Require more Proof of it, including myself. And that is WHY Dr. Raymond Bernard went to the Trouble to write a whole book about it, called: "The Hollow Earth." Yes, it might even be Out of Print by now; but, it had quite an Influence at one Time, before Satellites came along to "Prove him WRong" by taking millions of Pictures of the North Polar Regions, none of which show any Holes: beCause of that Cloud that King David spoke of in the Book of Isaiah, which Hides the Hole! {See: **"The New MAGNIFIED Version of ISAIAH in Plain English!"** B-044.}

12-11 [_] So, O Selected King, if the Hole is actually there, and is about 800 Miles in Diameter, would it not be Visible to Pilots in Airplanes?

12-12 [_] Well, the Hole could not be Visible to anyone in an Airplane: because Airplanes do not Cross Over the North Hole: beCause their Instruments do not Work in that Area: beCause of the Magnetic Fields, or whatever. Therefore, you cannot get a Ride Directly over the Hole, in spite of it being a Shorter Route to take from Germany to Alaska, for Example. However, even if you Deliberately went to Alaska in Search of the Hole, you could not easily Discover it: beCause the Earth Curves Inward as you Fly over it, and ever so Slightly: so that you would not Recognize it as anything but Normal Land and Water — that is, until you were well Inside of the Hole, where you could easily get Lost, and might even Imagine that you are Flying over Russia! Indeed, it is a Great Wilderness, with nothing to Identify it as the Paradise, until you get well into it, where you might Spot Herds of Woolly Mammoth Elephants grazing on Pine Trees, which, of course, would take you by Surprise! However, without Workable Instruments, you can easily Understand that you would soon not know which Way is Up, and which Way is Down, which would also be True for whomever is Chasing after you with a Limited Amount of Fuel, who would likely be *"Swallowed Up by the Earth,"* just as it is Written! Yes, it would be Suicidal for all such Ignorant People: beCause they would not know which Direction they should go to Return for more Fuel, once they were well Inside of the Hollow Earth, who would also be Greatly Spooked by those Woolly Mammoth Elephants and other Strange Creatures, who might also be Met by Hordes of Flying Saucers zipping all about, which would Naturally Lead them unto their own Deaths: beCause of not Watching the Gages very Carefully: beCause of the Excitement of it all, whereby they would Run Out of Fuel long after it is too Late to Turn Back, Safely. Therefore, it will Work like a Perfect Trap for the Serpent / Dragon Kingdom. †§

12-13 [_] O Selected King, it Sounds like God will have the Last Laugh. However, will it not be Possible for the Serpent Kingdom to send Refueling Planes along with the Fighter Planes, whereby they can Survive it?

12-14 [_] No, they will not be Prepared for that: beCause of Imagining that the "Escapees" cannot get Away from them, without Calculating what those Aliens might have Planned for them with their Flying Saucers. After all, God can Answer Prayers when he Wants to; and, in that Case, he will Want to, just to Fulfill the Prophecy. Therefore, the Earth will Swallow Up that Foolish Air Force; but, it will not be Reported in the Divided States of United Lies: beCause of being too Em-bare-assing.

— Chapter 13 —

The Great Eagle will Land on Mount Zion

13-01 [_] O Selected King, it is really Difficult for me to Believe that you are Serious. However, I keep Asking myself, "Why did he Write this Book, if he is not Serious?" And the Holy Spirit says: "He is Serious, and this is a very Serious Subject." Therefore, I have to keep Reading with a Capital R: beCause I have no Desire to go through the Great Tribulation.

13-02 [_] Well, if you Honestly have no Desire to go through the Great Tribulation, there is only ONE Way that you can Avoid it, and that is to Help other People to Escape, whereby you might also be Found Worthy to Escape. Yes, if you have Mercy on others, God may have Mercy on you, and thus make it Possible for you to Escape. However, if you do not Show Love and Compassion for other People, how can God Show Love and Compassion for you? Therefore, to Prove that you are a Loving Person with Compassion for others, you must Help me to Publish my Inspired Books, whereby all of the Believers might Learn about that Great Eagle, and at least Strive to Enter into Mount Zion, which is Reserved for HOLY People, only.

13-03 [_] O Selected King, you have Clearly Stated that you are NOT a Holy Man, yourself; and yet you seem to be Suggesting that you too will be Riding on the Back of that Great Eagle, rather than make a Sacrifice to Save the Holy Ones, if you know what I Mean?

13-04 [_] No, I have no Idea what you Mean.

13-05 [_] Well, O Selected King, you are otherwise known as the Colorful Peacock from Angel Ridge, King's Mountain, Kentucky, who is even more Subtle than any Snake who ever Lived, which is WHY you like to Peck on the Brains of Snakes, and also Tease their Tails, if you know what I Mean?

13-06 [_] No, I have no Idea what you Mean.

13-07 [_] Well, O Selected King, you can Find Out what I Mean by Studying: **"Mark Twain Races for the PRESIDENCY!" (The 2020 Presidential Candidates Desperately Need Some STRONG Undefeatable COMPETITION!) By The Worldwide People's Revolution!® Book 033.** Yes, the Answer is most Certainly in that Good Book; but, you Overlooked it, even as you should have: beCause it is Best that you do not Know what I Mean, lest you should be Grieved by it. However, not to Worry: beCause God is well Able to Raise you Up, and Set you Up on the Golden Throne within the Great World TEMPLE of PEACE, in Jerusalem. Moreover, if it were not so, I would have Told you. {See www.Amazon.com for: **"The Great World TEMPLE of PEACE!" (The Glory of Jerusalem Arises Again!), Book 017, plus: "The CONSTITUTION for the New RIGHTEOUS One-World GovernMINT!" (How all Peoples can get True Justice, and Celebrate the Great Year of JUBILEE!) By The Worldwide People's Revolution!®, Book 016, which is a Companion Book of: "The END of CONFUSION!" (The Great CELEBRATION of the Magnificent Wedding of the Most Humble Honest Nations, and the Grand Year of JUBILEE!) By The Worldwide People's Revolution!® Book 050.**}

13-08 [_] Well, it almost Sounds Biblical, and probably is Biblical; but, most People will not Recognize it as such: beCause of being Unfamiliar with the *Bible,* much less with *the Book of MORMON,* which makes it Perfectly Clear. {See www.Amazon.com for: **"The New MAGNIFIED Version of the Book of MORMON!" (The Story of the White and Dark Indians in the Americas!) By The Worldwide People's Revolution!**® Books 040A and 040B.}

13-09 [_] O Selected King, I must Confess that you Jumped Off of the Train Track in this Chapter, even though most of the Chapters also Jumped Off, as if God did not Want you to make everything Perfectly Clear within this Inspired Book. Indeed, it is perhaps your single Worst Book. However, other People, who Escape from the Great Tribulation: beCause of it, will be saying that it is your Best Book! Yes, they will say that they would have never Learned about Mount Zion, if it had not been for YOU, and especially for this Inspired Book, which I Promise to Help you to Publish, just for the Money, of course: beCause I Understand that I can Keep 90% of the Net Profits from the Sales. Therefore, I will also Encourage other People to Sell it for the same Reason, whereby it might be found Published in all Major Languages, Worldwide. However, it does Bother me to Think that few People will be Able to Understand it. †§‡

13-10 [_] Well, did you Check the Box for Verse 13-09? And will you Follow through with your Promise to Help Publish it? If not, I have no Idea HOW you will Escape from the Great Tribulation, since every "Escapee" must pass through my Office in Person with his or her own Personal Copy of this Book in his or her Hand: so that I can Inspect the Boxes that he or she Checked with X's. After all, if there are Snakes Lurking about, we must Discover them by the SURVEYS of their VALUES! Yes, those little Boxes are very Important Things to Consider: beCause they can make all of the Difference between "Salvation" and "Hellfire," you might say!

13-11 [_] O Elected King, I Swear to God that I have no Idea what you are Talking about. Can you not make yourself more Plain and Easy to Understand?

13-12 [_] Well, of course, I could; but, I am not going to: because I Want to Catch all of the Snakes who might Try to Sneak into Mount Zion without Passing their Tests. Indeed, can anything get more Plain than that? §

13-13 [_] O Selected King, if I have to Check all of the Boxes with Statements that I Agree with, I will have to Do some SERIOUS Studying, which is too Great of a Sacrifice for me: beCause I never did Like to Study Words very much.

13-14 [_] Well, you can Comfort yourself by the Fact that no Literature on this Earth gets any Better than my Literature, which makes it very Pleasant to Study with a Capital S. Guaranteed.

13-15 [_] O Selected King, it is just too Burdensome for me. My Eyes are not in Good Condition. I cannot read for very long.

13-16 [_] Well, in that Case, you should get someone to do the Reading for you, out loud, and not while you are half Asleep, nor Daydreaming. Yes, it Requires Concentration.

(HOW the True Church will Escape from the Great Tribulation!)

— Chapter 14 —

Will Alma and Abinadi be there when we get there?

14-01 [_] Yes, is the Answer to that Question. However, you might Ask, "IF the Book of Mormon is PHONY, HOW could they be there?" Well, that Mystery is Revealed in: **"The New MAGNIFIED Version of the Book of MORMON!" (The Story of the White and Dark Indians in the Americas!) By The Worldwide People's Revolution!®** Book 040B. Yes, not only that, but many Mysteries are Revealed within that Good Book, which is most Definitely Inspired by GOD. †§‡

14-02 [_] O Selected King, are YOU a Mormon, or a Latter-day Sinner??

14-03 [_] Well, I am a Covert Latter-day Saint, for Sure; but, you would not Know it: beCause I am Highly Camouflaged, even as I should be: beCause there is no other Way to bring about this Great Work and such a Marvelous Wonder, so as to Save the Honest Sheeps of the Good Shepherd, who will be Gathered Up from among all of the Nations for the Great Wedding of the Nations Celebration, in Jerusalem, in the Great World TEMPLE of PEACE! Yes, it will be a most Marvelous Thing to Behold when Jesus Christ Appears, in Person, when he Suddenly Comes to his Temple, Unexpectedly. So, be Sure to have your White Under Garment on.

14-04 [_] O Elected King, I must Confess that God does Things in Strange Ways; but, this is the Strangest of all: beCause there is no Way that you could be a Latter-day Saint of any Kind nor Color: beCause you do not even Observe Sunday as the Sabbath Day. †§‡

14-05 [_] Well, that Part is True: beCause God did not Change his Sabbath Day, or else he would not be the same, both Yesterday, Today, and Forever. Therefore, whatever I Do, I Do it with a Good Purpose, or else I would not Do it.

14-06 [_] O Selected King, I Think that you should Reconsider Joining the Church, again: beCause it is the one and only True Church of Jesus Christ. {See: **"Which Church is the True Church?"**}

14-07 [_] Well, his True Church is made up of Holy People, only. Therefore, there is no Way that I can Join it, being Unholy.

14-08 [_] Oo Mas'er Twaan, if'n ye iz not Hooleez, noo wun els iz.

14-09 [_] Well, O Nigger Jim, that is simply not True: beCause many People have Pure Minds; but, not Pure Bodies: beCause they do not Realize that it Requires BOTH a Pure Mind, Clean Bowels, and a Purified Spirit, which can only be Purified by FIRE, by the Baptism of the Holy Spirit, which is a REAL Fire. However, it does not Consume the People who are SUBMERSED in it. ‡

14-10 [_] O Selected King, if we have to be Baptized with Fire before we can go to Mount Zion, you can Count me OUT: beCause that is a little too Spooky for me.

14-11 [_] Trust me, it will be a Wonderful Experience; and then, after that, Multitudes of People will have to Confess that at least that Part of the Bible is True, huh?

14-12 [_] Well, O Elected King, I will tell you right now that I am NOT Looking Forward to it: beCause it is far too Spooky for me.

14-13 [_] Well, the Reason it is so Spooky to you, is beCause you cannot Explain HOW it can be Done; but, like all Supernatural Things, it is not Meant to be Explained, except to say that GOD did it: beCause only some Great Powerful God could Baptize an entire Church with Fire, and not Burn it up, nor even Singe a single Hair on anyone's Head! However, if any Unclean Person is among them, who has not Purified his or her own Bowels by Means of much Fasting and Praying, that Person is likely to be Consumed by the Fire! Therefore, that could Prove to be a little Spooky for them, and Especially if they are SPIES.

14-14 [_] O Elected King, I dare say that you have Lost your Right Mind, if you Think that God is going to Baptize any of these Filthy Americans with FIRE, seeing that they are Gluttonous HOGS, Stinking Skunks, Poisonous Snakes, Liars, Deceivers, Hypocrites, and Ignorant IDIOTS! Yes, they are the Worst of Hypocrites, who say that they Love God, while Hating those Muslims, who are more Righteous than they are, just beCause there are X-amount of BAD Muslims, who Accept the Koran Literally, rather than Study the Book that Muhammad Recommended, which is the *Holy Bible,* which he Referred to as "the Book." †§‡

14-15 [_] Well, it will be Interesting to See who Actually takes the Wings of a Great Eagle and Flies Away into the Wilderness with John, the Beloved Disciple, who is still with us.

14-16 [_] O Selected King, are you Kidding us? John must have Died at least a thousand 700 Years Ago!

14-17 [_] Well, if that is True, how is it that I could See him, in Person? Indeed, I Believe that he is still Alive and Well. (See *John 21.*)

14-18 [_] O Elected King, will John Guide the Great Eagle into the Wilderness?

(HOW the True Church will Escape from the Great Tribulation!)

— Chapter 15 —

Jesus Tells us what to Do, himself!

15-01 [_]

Jesus Tells us what to Do, continued ...

(HOW the True Church will Escape from the Great Tribulation!)

— Chapter 16 —

The Conclusion

16-01 [_] O Selected King of **The Worldwide People's Revolution!®**, whatever Happened to Chapter 15? Did you Forget it?

16-02 [_] Well, I was about to Write it; but, the Holy Spirit said: "These People are not yet Ready for it. Besides that, they Need to Suffer Longer, just to come to their Right Senses." Therefore, we will have to leave it at that.

16-03 [_] O Selected King, I do wish to God that I Knew for Sure that you are the Man with the Spirit of Elijah: beCause, if you are, we are Relying on you to Save us. Therefore, suppose someone Assassinates you — what should we Do?

16-04 [_] Well, it is not something that you have to Worry about: beCause most People will just Naturally Think that I am CRAZY, and therefore Harmless.

16-05 [_] So, O Elected King, are you saying that you are NOT Harmless? Can we not Trust you to be Harmless?

16-06 [_] Well, you probably Remember the Hebrew Story about King Nebuchadnezzar, and how his Nature was Changed: beCause God was Managing his Life. Well, it is the same Way with me, since he is Obviously Managing my Life. Therefore, if I am Changed into a Tyrant, do not Blame me for it. After all, the Masses of People could simply OBEY the Great Truths that I have Revealed, and it would be Impossible for me to be Transformed into a Tyrant. Moreover, I have no Idea what a Tyrant might Do, since I have never been one. †§‡

16-07 [_] O Selected King, are you Sure that too much Bible Study has not Driven you Insane? Would it not be much Better for all of us, if we just TRASHED the Bible and the Book of Morons? After all, both of them, and the Koran, can easily be Proven to be PHONY, and just as Fake as Noah's Ark, which could not have Held even one-hundredth enough Fresh Water for all of those Animals for 14 Months!

16-08 [_] Well, I would say that I might be a little too Tired to be doing any Writing: because it is passed Midnight; but, I wanted to Finish this Book this Week, just so that I could say that I Wrote one Book per Week for the past Month, which is in Fact the Case, for whatever it is Worth, which only the Man with the Spirit of Elijah could Do: beCause, without the Guidance of the Holy Spirit, how could it be Done?

16-09 [_] O Selected King, anyone with a Fertile Imagination could easily Do what you have Done, just as long as he or she did not Eat very much, whereby his or her Brains might Function Correctly. †§‡

63

16-10 [_] Well, if that is True, why do you not Do it, just to Prove it? After all, you probably know your Bible fairly well. In Fact, I will leave the remainder of this Page Blank, just for you to Write your Most Inspired Words for us to Read at **"The Great Worldwide TELEVISED Court HEARING,"** just in Case you make any such False Statements during the Future, and have nothing to Support your False Claims. {See www.Amazon.com for: **"LIGHTNING STRIKES Versus Lightning Bugs and Impotent Fireflies!" (A Memorial Photo Album of some Real American Heroes!)**, Book 072, which is a Companion Book of: **"The BEST of CAPITALISM!" (Corrections for "LIGHTNING STRIKES Versus Lightning Bugs and Impotent Fireflies!")**, Book 073, plus: **"The Environmentalists' Paradise!" (How almost Everyone could be Living in a Beautiful Manmade Paradise!)**, Book 035, plus: **"Terrorists Beware that your Days are Numbered!" (HOW to Bring those Terrorist Attacks to a Screeching HALT!)**, Book 043, plus: **"SWANGKEENOMIKS Rules the Roost!" (How all People can Prosper in a RIIT WAA, and STOP Polluting the Earth with Capitalist TRASH!) By The Worldwide People's Revolution!®** Book 039. NOTE: This Book and the last 3 in the List, above, were written during the past Month. Therefore, just Try to Match them with something Better, if you can.}

The Enticement,

Our Selected King tells HOW the True Church will Escape from the Great Tribulation, and Avoid the Dreaded Mark of the Beast, even as he, himself will also Avoid it, and Fly Away on the Wings of a Great Eagle, as the Book of Revelation puts it. Yes, Pray that you are also Accounted Worthy to Escape: beCause there is a Way, and NOT by Means of the so-called Rapture, which is Superstitious Religious Nonsense, pure and simple! Indeed, wherever the Carcasses are, there the Vultures will be Gathered Together to Feast on them who Mock the Divine Revelations of Almighty God, some of which can be found within this Inspired Book for your Education, Entertainment and Enlightenment. Therefore, do not Deprive yourself of it, unto your own Great Shame, O Lady Doubtfulness.

(HOW the True Church will Escape from the Great Tribulation!)

A Long List of other Fascinating Literature by the same Inspired Author

[ ] 40-01 — **"LIGHTNING Versus the Lightning Bug!"** (HOW almost Everyone can become Moderately RICH, without Telling Any Lies nor Selling Any Trash!) Book 001.

[ ] 40-02 — **"What is WRong with those Professing Christians?"** (A Self-Examination of the Heart of the Body of Good Government!) Book 002.

[ ] 40-03 — **"For the Love of Money!"** (The Strange Things that People Say and Do to Get more Money!) Book 003.

[ ] 40-04 — **"HOW to Prepare for CLIMATE CHANGES!"** (The Wisest Plan for Mankind to Follow!) Book 004.

[ ] 40-05 — **"Why do I have to be Surrounded by CRAZY PEOPLE!"** (Do almost all People Feel like they are Surrounded by CRAZY People??) Book 005.

[ ] 40-06 — **"The Washington Journal is a FARCE! (C-SPAN Managers are not very WISE!)** Book 006. (This Book has lots of Good Humor.)

[ ] 40-07 — **"The PRAYERS of PUMPKINHEADS!"** (Even God Needs a Little Humor to Cheer himself Up!) Book 007. (Some of it is for Adults only.)

[ ] 40-08 — **"A Sound Argument for Masters and Servants!"** (WHY Everyone Needs a Good Master, and every Master Needs Good Obedient Servants!) Book 008.

[ ] 40-09 — **"WHY are some Preachers so POOR?"** (HOW almost all Preachers could Get Moderately RICH, without Preaching any Outlandish LIES!) Book 009.

[ ] 40-10 — **"GOOD NEWS for REBEL WOMEN!"** (HOW almost all Wives can become Moderately RICH without Leaving their Homes! Guaranteed!) Book 010.

[ ] 40-11 — **"The Low Court of Supreme Injustices is Brought to Trial!"** (The Worldwide People's Revolution!® Butts Heads with the United States Supreme Court, with or without their Black Robes of Hypocrisies and Lies!) Book 011. (This Inspired Book contains the Famous *Declaration of Interdependence,* which is a Must Read. It also contains the Correct Wording for the Placard on the Statue of Liberty.)

[ ] 40-12 — **"The Right Design for Living!"** (A List of Great Advantages for Building Beautiful Planned City States!) Book 012. (This Book contains many Important Drawings, as well as HOW to Save hundreds of Trillions of Dollars by Building Swanky Fortresses, and Living in Peace within them. It is a Companion Book of Book 011, which contains many more Great Advantages for Fortresses.)

[_] 40-13 — **"The Gospel According to The Worldwide People's Revolution!® " (The Good News from the Most Modern Perspective!)** Book 013. (This Book contains the Famous Sermon of Jonah to the Ninevites, whereby 120,000 People Repented in Sackcloth and Ashes! Do not Miss Out on it.)

[_] 40-14 — **"Poverty Hunger Riots Strikes Brutalities Election Deceptions and Civil Wars!" (The High Price that we Earthlings have Paid for Leaving the Good Land!)** Book 014.

[_] 40-15 — **"Seven Great Armies of Working Soldiers!" (HOW to Provide a Way for Everyone to WORK: so as to Eliminate Poverty, Crimes, Drug Abuses, Prisons and Unnecessary Taxes!)** Book 015. (This Book contains a True Life Story when I was in the Army.)

[_] 40-16 — **"The CONSTITUTION for the New RIGHTEOUS One-World GovernMint!" (HOW all Peoples can get True Justice, and Celebrate the Great Year of JUBILEE!)** Book 016.

[_] 40-17 — **"The Great World TEMPLE of PEACE!" (The Glory of Jerusalem Arises Again!) By The Worldwide People's Revolution!®** Book 017.

[_] 40-18 — **"The Swanky Associations of Working Soldiers!" (A Fascinating Collection of Various Kinds of Voluntary Working Soldiers!)** Book 018. (There will be thousands of Associations for all Kinds of Occupations, which will Specialize in Fine Arts — such as Hand-carved Leather-bound Books. See **"LIGHTNING STRIKES Versus Lightning Bugs!"** Book 074, for a Good Example.)

[_] 40-19 — **"GLORIOUS Swanky Hotels Castles and Fortresses!" (Beautiful Planned City States for WISE Intelligent Well-Educated People with Common Sense and Good Understanding!)** Book 019. (This Book contains many Rough Drawings, which could be Greatly Improved upon by someone who Knows the Art, and has the Correct Computer Programs for doing it.)

[_] 40-20 — **"Are you a Jobless Graduate of the SKQL uv FQLZ?" (HOW to Get a GOUD EJUKAASHUN without Robbing the Bank!)** Book 020. (This Inspired Book contains the New MAGNIFIED Version {NMV} of *First Corinthians 13,* plus: HOW to Produce Pure Living Water!)

[_] 40-21 — **"The LUSCIOUS All-Mineral Organic Method of Gardening!" (HOW to Grow DELICIOUS Satisfying Foods for Potential Kingz and Kweenz in Beautiful Swanky PALACES!)** Book 021. (This Book Explains HOW to make a Flood-proof Garden, while Trapping the Rainwater.)

[_] 40-22 — **"Did God or Satan Ordain Medical Doctors?" (Ask Huck Finn and/or Nigger Jim: because neither Tom Sawyer nor Judge Thatcher would Know!)** Book 022. (This Inspired Book Reveals HOW to Prevent Common Colds, and has a Special Chapter that Explains what a True "Nigger" IS. Surprise yourself!)

(HOW the True Church will Escape from the Great Tribulation!)

[_] 40-23 — **"The BIG White OUTHOUSE on the Not-so-Biblical Capitol DUNGHILL!" (The Chief Sins of the Divided States of United Lies!) By The Worldwide People's Revolution!® Book 023.** (This Book contains Special Words that most People have never Heard! Surprise yourself again!)

[_] 40-24 — **"The Public School of IGNERUNT FQLZ!" (HOW we have been GRAATLEE DISEEVD by Capitalism!) Book 024.** (This Book Teaches Children HOW to "Reed and Riit in Funetik Ingglish in just wun Daa!" You should Challenge your Frendz and Naaberz with it.)

[_] 40-25 — **"In thu Beeginingz uv Thingz!" (Thu Kreeaashun Stooree frum thu Beegining!) Book 025.** {The Cover Photo shows a Picture of a Golden Supootaa (Sapote), which not one Person in a Million has ever Tasted: because it does not Ship very well, in spite of it being one of the most Sweetest Pleasant Fruits known to Mankind, which must Ripen on the Tree to be Extremely Good, after it is Grown Properly by **"The LUSCIOUS All-Mineral Organic Method of Gardening!"** Book 021, which Means that the Topsoil must have all of the Proper Minerals in it. Remember the Grapes of Eschol, which the Children of Israel brought back from the Promised Land in the *Book of Joshua,* which Required 2 Strong Men to Carry just one Cluster! See the Fascinating Photos in: **"Orgimmick Gardening at its Best!" (HOW to Grow Delicious Satisfying Foods without a 10-Million-Dollar Investment!) By The Worldwide People's Revolution!® Book 079.**}

[_] 40-26 — **"God Speaks and the Whole World Listens!" (Fire on the Mountain from the Burning Bush by the Spirit of Truths!) Book 026.** (This Powerful Book contains the Best Noah Story of all of the Books, including that of Gilgamesh the Great of Ancient Babylon!)

[_] 40-27 — **"Does a Good Soldier have to be a MURDERER?" (Seven Great Swanky Armies of Voluntary Working Soldiers!) By The Worldwide People's Revolution!® Book 027.** (Chapter 03 contains a True Life Story about a Dog Pile, which happened to me when I was just 10 Years Old.)

[_] 40-28 — **"Thu Nq MAGNUFIID Verzhun uv Thu PROVERBZ uv KING SOLUMUN in Plaan Ingglish!" (The Understandable Version of the Famous Proverbs of King Solomon in Plain English!) Book 028.** (This Marvelous Book MAGNIFIES each Proverb unto the Glory of the Great God of Inspiration, which is taken from the Original 4,000-page Book, which was written in less than 2 Months by the GIFT of Inspiration, which also contains the Famous Proverbs of Queen Izubelu!)

[_] 40-29 — **"UNLIMITED ENERJEE 99 Percent Pollutions Free!" (HOW to Obtain FREE ElecTrickery, Worldwide!) By The Worldwide People's Revolution!® Book 029.** (This Book contains the Jackson Brower Suicide, among many other Fascinating Subjects.)

[_] 40-30 — **"FREEDUM uv SPEECH!" (U Speshoul Maguzeen uv Onist Upinyunz!) Book 030-0001,** which contains the Great Advantages for Using Swanky Mulching Rocks in an All-Mineral Organic Garden, plus Baptism by Fire and Speaking in Foreign Languages! It is a Must Read. The Cover Photo shows a Portion of the Author's Marbleous Indian Countertop or Food Bar, which is just one Example of what you can also have in your own **"Beautiful Swanky PALACES!"** if you have the Honesty, Faith, Hope, Trust, Love, Patience, Persistence,

Cooperation and OBEDIENCE that are Required for True Prosperity! Therefore, Ejukaat yourself, and you will be Glad that you did!

[_] 40-31 — **"A Sure Cure for GUN VIOLENCE!" (HOW TO STOP GANG WARS and CRIMINAL SHOOTINGS!) By The Worldwide People's Revolution!®** Book 031. {The Cover Photo shows a Picture of a Short Shotgun, which is Fully Loaded with Double 00 Shells, and is Ready for any Tax Master who might Attempt to Steal the Retirement Home, who never moved a Finger to Help Build the Rock Houses, whereby we moved more than 66,666,666 Pounds by Hand, whose Property was Cunningly Stolen by that False Anti-Christ WICKED Cover-up Government, which allowed Bankers to Rob us of 30 Years of Hard Labor and more than 300,000 dollars-worth of Investments in our Uncommon American Farm, which is Explained in: **"LIGHTNING STRIKES Versus Lightning Bugs!" (HOW you can Become Moderately RICH, without Telling any Lies nor Selling any Trash!) By The Worldwide People's Revolution!®** Book 074, which contains many Photographs with Profound Explanations! Do not be left out in the Darkness of Ignorance. Get Informed, now: beCause, **"The Great False Economy is now DEBUNKED!"** Book 053.}

[_] 40-32 — **"AIIRMWVC and Reasonable Solutions!" (Aliens, Illegal Immigrants, Refugees, Migrant Workers and other Victims of Capitalism!) By The Worldwide People's Revolution!®** Book 032. (This Inspired Book contains *the New MAGNIFIED Version of Job 33*.)

[_] 40-33 — **"Mark Twain Races for the PRESIDENCY!" (The 2020 Presidential Candidates Desperately Need Some STRONG Undefeatable COMPETITION!) By The Worldwide People's Revolution!®** Book 033. {This Book contains a Part of my Autobiography, and my Personal Answers to the Questions in **"The Complete SURVEYS of our VALUES!" (SURVEYS of Religious Spiritual Political Governmental Sexual Social Moral Economic Business Labor Habitual and Miscellaneous VALUES!)** Book 059. It also contains many Black and White Photographs.}

[_] 40-34 — **"ECCLESIASTES UNCOVERED!" (The New MAGNIFIED Version of Ecclesiastes and the Song of Solomon in Plain English!)** Book 034. (This is the Book that contains the Famous Sayings for *"There is a Time to be Born, and a Time to Die ..."* which has been Greatly Magnified!)

[_] 40-35 — **"The Environmentalists' Paradise!" (HOW almost Everyone could be Living in a Beautiful Manmade Paradise!) By The Worldwide People's Revolution!®** Book 035. (This Book contains the NMV of *Psalm 48,* which will Amaze you, O Lady Doubtfulness!)

[_] 40-36 — **"The Seven Basic Spiritual Building Blocks of LIFE!" (Faith Hope Trust Love Patience Persistence and Obedience!)** Book 036. (This Book contains the Mockingbird's Version of *Hebrews 11,* plus the NMV of *First Corinthians 13,* among many other "Goodies.")

[_] 40-37 — **"DIETS!" (A Reasonable Solution for the "Eternal Controversy"!) By The Worldwide People's Revolution!®** Book 037.

[_] 40-38 — **"The Nature of CAPITALISM!" (A List of the EVILS of CAPITALISM!)** Book 038.

[ ] 40-39 — **"SWANGKEENOMIKS Rules the Roost!" (HOW all People can Prosper in a RIIT WAA, and STOP Polluting the Earth with Capitalist TRASH!) By The Worldwide People's Revolution!® Book 039.** (The Cover Photo shows a Portion of our Retirement Home, before the 5,000+ square-feet Concrete Roof was Installed, after moving more than 66 Million Pounds by Hand!)

[ ] 40-40 — **"The New MAGNIFIED Version of The Book of MORMON!" (The Story of the White and Dark Indians in the Americas!)** Book 040, which comes in 2 Volumes of about 500 Pages, each. The Cover Photo on the First Volume shows the Queen of England's Golden Coach, and the Cover Photo on the Second Volume shows one of many Polished Spanish Marble Walls in our Selected King's Retirement Home, which is worth a thousand dollars per square yard, which is another Example of what you can also have, if you simply OBEY your Righteous KING! All such Marble is very Inspiring. No one could Study it for very long without Believing in a Great Creator God. The Picture does not do it Justice. You would have to See it in Person, and Wash it with Pure Water to bring Out the Beauty.

[ ] 40-41 — **"The GREAT Worldwide TELEVISED Court HEARING!" (That Great Meeting of the Most Intelligent and Wel-Ejukaatid Miindz!) By The Worldwide People's Revolution!® Book 041.** {This is the Book that the World has long been Waiting for: beCause it will Overthrow the Evil Empires, and make it Possible to Establish **"The New RIGHTEOUS One-World Government!" (HOW to Establish a Righteous One-World Government without Going to WAR!) By The Worldwide People's Revolution!® Book 056.** This is the Greatest Idea since the Invention of the Light Bulb, Guaranteed!}

[ ] 40-42 — **"The Secret City of the Great King!" (HOW the True Church will Escape from the Great Tribulation!) By The Worldwide People's Revolution!® Book 042.** (Be Sure to Inform your Friends, Relatives and Naaberz about this Wonderful Book: beCause they might also Want to Escape!)

[ ] 40-43 — **"Terrorists Beware that your Days are Numbered!" (HOW to Bring those Terrorist Attacks to a Screeching HALT!) By The Worldwide People's Revolution!® Book 043.** (This Book also contains the Fascinating Book of LEHI, which has now been Restored!) †‡

[ ] 40-44 — **"The New MAGNIFIED Version of ISAIAH in Plain English!" (The Understandable Version of the Book of Isaiah!)** Book 044. (The Cover Photo shows a Swanky Potato and Avocado Salad with Sweet Peas and Corn, among other "Secret" Ingredients, which are Revealed within the Book. Remember that you can read many Words for Free in the Book Previews on Amazon.com.usa.)

[ ] 40-45 — **"HOW to Become a HOLY Man!" (40 Good Reasons WHY People Should FAST and PRAY!)** Book 045, which is a Companion Book of:

[ ] 40-46 — **"The Proper RULES for FASTING!" (The Complete Instruction Manual for True Repentance!) By The Worldwide People's Revolution!® Book 046,** which is a Companion Book of the above mentioned Book, which contains a True Life Story about an Old Black Mare called Lucy, who Fasted for 30 Days without Food nor Water, who was Physiologically "Born Again," as Jesus might say. See the Full Details in: **"The New**

MAGNIFIED Version of The GOOD NEWS According to Saint JOHN!" (The Gospel According to Saint John Zebedee Boanerges in Plain English!) Book 062, which contains many Inspiring Photographs with Explanations!

[_] 40-47 — **"Are Americans the Most STUPID People who ever Lived?" (HOW Working People can PROSPER and Live in PEACE Under the Rulership of a RIGHTEOUS KING!) By The Worldwide People's Revolution!®** Book 047. (The Cover Photo shows a large Portion of the Author's Living Room Floor, which is worth 100,000$, which is just another Good Example of what you can also have, just for Loving and Obeying your Elected King!)

[_] 40-48 — **"An Amazing Collection of Wit and Wisdom!" (The Marvelous Tale of the Colorful Peacock from Angel Ridge, and the Strong Rope of Everlasting Hope!) By The Worldwide People's Revolution!®** Book 048. (The Cover Photo shows a Book Display, which will be Greatly Enhanced during the Future, when all 350+ Inspired Books are on Display in a Swanky Truth-brary, as Opposed to the Public LIE-brary.)

[_] 40-49 — **"Justifications for Capitalizations!" (WHY The Worldwide People's Revolution!® Defies the School of Fools by Capitalizing LOVE and HATE!)** Book 049.

[_] 40-50 — **"The END of CONFUSION!" (The Great CELEBRATION of the Magnificent Wedding of the Most Humble Honest Nations, and the Grand Year of JUBILEE!) By The Worldwide People's Revolution!®** Book 050. (Just Try to Visualize those **"Seven Great Swanky Armies of Voluntary Working Soldiers"** Marching through the Valley of Megiddo, being Dressed in their Colorful Robes, while the Band Plays *The Battle Hymn of the Republic,* and the Choirs Sing the Praises of the Great KING of Kings! What a Sight and Sound that will be, which will be Climaxed in **"The Great World TEMPLE of PEACE,"** when the Nations will get Married, along with our Elected King! Come one, come all to **"The Great Worldwide TELEVISED Court HEARING,"** by Means of your Wide Flat-screen TVs, whereby you might Learn WHY, WHEN and HOW!) †‡

[_] 40-51 — **"The Loathsome Burdens of the Independent Jackasses!" (A New Civilized Approach for Quietly Solving our Massive Problems!) By The Worldwide People's Revolution!®** Book 051. (Just Think about the Multitude of almost Worthless Meetings of the Minds, who Strained themselves to Think of Reasonable Solutions for our Massive Problems, who sometimes even Prayed to God for Help; but, the Solutions have been here for no less than 40 Years — Thanks to the Spirit of Inspiration from GOD!)

[_] 40-52 — **"Are we Tax Slaves of a Lower Order than those Lying Edomites!" (HOW to be Liberated from all Slavery, Worldwide!) By The Worldwide People's Revolution!®** Book 052. {This Inspired Book once had another Title and Author, which was not Acceptable by Amazon, which has now been Restored in all of its Glory, and is Published by more Trustworthy People, who are not Afraid of Controversies, nor of: **"The Swanky Sword of Divine Truths!" (The Most Powerful Weapon in the Whole Universe!) By The Worldwide People's Revolution!®** Book 067.}

[_] 40-53 — **"The Great False Economy is now DEBUNKED!" (Adolf Hitler had a much Better Economic System!) By The Worldwide People's Revolution!®** Book 053. (Trust me,

(HOW the True Church will Escape from the Great Tribulation!)

Adolf was no Saint; but, during the Day of God's Judgment, he will be Justified, while his Anti-Christ Opponents will be Condemned: beCause they Refused to Attend a Worldwide Radio Debate with Adolf Hitler, whose Arguments will Stand Up during the Day of Judgment, which would have Prevented World War 2, and thus Saved the Lives of no less than 60 Million People! Likewise, we Tax Slaves must now Act more Wisely, and DEMAND **"The Great Worldwide TELEVISED Court HEARING,"** Book 041, whereby we might Save the World from that Dreadful Battle of Megiddo, called *Armageddon!* Yes, the Ball is now in YOUR Hands, my Potential Friend or Enemy, and you are now Responsible for it. Therefore, do not Shirk your Duty as a Free Citizen; but, Help us to Spread this Message far and wide, whereby the Masses of People will be Demanding The GWTCH, and thus Prevent another far more Dreadful and Hateful World WAR!)

[_] 40-54 — **"The UGLY Scarred Dishonest Face of Poor Old Miserable UNCLE SAM!" (A Memorial Day Legacy!) By The Worldwide People's Revolution!®** Book 054. {NOTE: This Inspired Book was also Suppressed by Amazon, who will be most Ashamed of themselves if they do not Un-suppress it during the Future: beCause it will also be Published by People of Greater Faith, who Know for a Fact that it is the TRUTH! Therefore, just be Patient.}

[_] 40-55 — **"The United States of the Whole World!" (A True Global Economy for the Masses of Working People!) By The Worldwide People's Revolution!®** Book 055. (This Inspired Book contains many Colored Photographs with Explanations. It is a Good Book to Publish in Foreign Nations, who are not so Blinded by their Pride, who can See the Mountain of Lies much Better at a Distance from them: beCause of not being a Part of the American Corruption.) †‡

[_] 40-56 — **"The New RIGHTEOUS One-World Government!" (HOW to Establish a Righteous One-World Government without Going to WAR!) By The Worldwide People's Revolution!®** Book 056. (This is a KEY Book, which everyone should Study Carefully and Prayerfully.)

[_] 40-57 — **"Those Ridiculous Contradictions within the Holy Bible!" (HOW to Read the Mutilated Bible with an Open Mind!) By The Worldwide People's Revolution!®** Book 057. (Many Professing "Christians" Falsely Claim that their so-called *"Holy Bibles"* do not Contain any Contradictions, being "the Infallible Inspired Word of the Living God," but, without the Capitalized Words, and without Explaining just WHY there are more than 200 Contradictory Versions of it! This Book Reveals how to Deal with those Biblical Problems, and come to Understand WHY God Allowed it to Happen for the Truth's Sake. Trust me, you have never Heard this Explanation before now.)

[_] 40-58 — **"The Divided States of United Lies!" (The so-called "United States of North America" in Disguise!) By The Worldwide People's Revolution!®** Book 058. {NOTE: This is perhaps the most Referred to Book among all of the Books by our Selected King; but, that does not Mean that it is his Best Book by any Means, which is Well Camouflaged: so that it will Survive the Test of Time, even if the others are BURNED by the Anti-Christ Followers of Satan, who are Possession Worshipers of the Worst Kind, who Seek to Justify American Lies, rather than Quickly Confess them, and thus Escape from their Self-made Prison of Propagandish Lies! Just be Perfectly Honest, and you will have no Problem with any of our Literature.}

[_] 40-59 — **"The Complete SURVEYS of our VALUES!" (SURVEYS of Religious Spiritual Political Governmental Sexual Social Moral Economic Business Labor Habitual and Miscellaneous VALUES!) By The Worldwide People's Revolution!®** Book 059. {NOTE: According to our Selected King, every Potential Leader in the World must Fill Out and File those Surveys on the Internet for everyone to Study, whereby the Best People might be Elected by those Wise People who have also Filled Out the Complete Surveys of their own Values, whereby they will be Qualified to VOTE. Otherwise, they will not be Qualified to Vote, which will Eliminate a LOT of Wasted Money on Election Deceptions, while at the same Time it will Educate a lot of Ignorant People, who Desperately Need to Study that Inspired Book before Voting for another Dimwitcrat, Reprobate, or Independent Jackass!}

[_] 40-60 — **"HOW to Get our PRIORITIES in ORDER!" (The Glories of Democracy; and, Does DEMON-ocracy have its Priorities in Order?) By The Worldwide People's Revolution!®** Book 060. This Book will need to be Re-written by a Collective Group of Wise People, who will Contribute their True Life Stories during the Future, when they Wake Up and come to their Right Senses with the Prodigal Son of *Luke 15*. See:

[_] 40-61 — **"The New MAGIFIED Version of The GOOD NEWS According to Saint LUKE!" (The Magnified Gospel of Saint Luke in Plain English!)** Book 061, which is by Far the Best Version of that Gospel on the Earth, which has no Rivals at all among the other 200+ Versions. Guaranteed!

[_] 40-62 — **"The New MAGNIFIED Version of The GOOD NEWS According to Saint JOHN!" (The Gospel According to Saint John Zebedee Boanerges in Plain English!)** Book 062, which also has no Rivals among all of the other Versions: beCause this is no Translation of anything; but, it is the Inspired Words of the Living God, which were Revealed by the Holy Spirit, who has not Died.

[_] 40-63 — **"The New MAGNIFIED Version of the Book of ACTS!" (The Understandable Version of the Acts of the Apostles in Plain English!) By The Worldwide People's Revolution!®** Book 063. (This Inspired Book makes it Understandable WHY the Jews Hated the Apostles so much. You will have to Read it to Believe it.)

[_] 40-64 — **"The New MAGNIFIED Version of the PSALMS of King David!" (The Understandable Version of the Famous Psalms in Plain English!)** Book 064. You will be Amazed!

[_] 40-65 — **"A List of FAIR Swanky Wages!" (The Equitable Wage System!) By The Worldwide People's Revolution!®** Book 065. (All Hardworking People will LOVE this Good Book!)

[_] 40-66 — **"Beautiful Swanky PALACES!" (A New Concept in Living Habits — Swanky Palaces for Poor People!) By The Worldwide People's Revolution!®** Book 066. (You have no Idea what a "Swanky Palace" IS, unless you have read this Unique Book.)

[_] 40-67 — **"The Swanky Sword of Divine Truths!" (The Most Powerful Weapon in the Whole Universe!)** Book 067. (The very Reason that our Selected King has no Rivals is beCause

(HOW the True Church will Escape from the Great Tribulation!)

of the Swanky Sword of Divine Truths, which no one can Defeat by any Means. Therefore, you Need to have it on your own Side, whereby no one can Defeat your Arguments! Be Strong, be Brave, have Faith and put on the Whole Armor of GOD!)

[_] 40-68 — **"Has your Life become Extremely Complicated?" (HOW to Live a SIMPLE Life!) By The Worldwide People's Revolution!® Book 068.** (Many People are not even Aware of just how Complicated their Lives are, until suddenly they are ready to Commit Suicide! It is Best to Prevent all such Evil Things, and this Book tells HOW.)

[_] 40-69 — **"The IDEAL Place to Live!" (HOW to Discover the Ideal Place to Live!) Book 069.**

[_] 40-70 — **"Our Elected King Who Speaks Out!" (It is High Time for some Sane Person to Get Control of this Insane World!) By The Worldwide People's Revolution!® Book 070.** (This Inspired Book contains a Special Speech that is Addressed to both Houses of the Congress in Washington. You will Love it, O Man of Greater Faith!)

[_] 40-71 — **"How GAY is GOD?" (Oh the Wonders of it all when it ALL Hangs Out!) Book 071.** (Do not Judge the Book, until you have Carefully "Red" all of it. You will be Surprised by the Truths!)

[_] 40-72 — **"LIGHTNING STRIKES Versus Lightning Bugs and Impotent Fireflies!" (A Memorial Photo Album of some Real American Heroes!) By The Worldwide People's Revolution!® Book 072.** (NOTE: This Book is Unique among all of the Books by our Selected King: beCause he did not get to Proof-read it before the Computer Crashed. It just Happened to be Saved on a Computer Chip before the Computer Crashed, and therefore it was Saved in PDF. But, the Corrections did not get made, which makes it a Special Collector's Item, which has more than 100 Colored Photos, which was what Caused the Crash.) †‡

[_] 40-73 — **"The BEST of CAPITALISM!" (Corrections for: "LIGHTNING STRIKES Versus Lightning Bugs and Impotent Fireflies!") Book 073.** (It is a completely new Book, except for those Corrections; and it is one of the Best Books in the World, which all Honest People will Love.)

[_] 40-74 — **"LIGHTNING STRIKES Versus Lightning Bugs!" (HOW you can Become Moderately RICH, without Telling any Lies nor Selling any Trash!) By The Worldwide People's Revolution!® Book 074**, which is the Perfection of all of the Lightning Striking Books, which is Recommended above all others for Mass Production: beCause it stands the Best Chance of being a Real Winner, just after this Book that you are now Reading, which has a Magnetizing Title!

[_] 40-75 — **"What are the Punishments for Dietary Sins?" (Have we Served ourselves Well at the Tables of our Lusts?) Book 075.** (This Book is too Controversial to be Published at this Time. Be very Patient until it is Available: beCause it is HOT!)

[_] 40-76 — "What is WRong with those CRAZY CHRISTIANS?" (A Self-Examination of the Heart of the Body of Good Government!) By The Worldwide People's Revolution!® Book 076.

[_] 40-77 — "The Gospel According to our Elected King!" (The Good News from the Most Modern Perspective!) Book 077. (This is perhaps the Best Book that you will Discover on Amazon, which contains the Famous Sermon that Jonah gave to the Ninevites, plus a very Special Sermon by Jesus Christ, himself!)

[_] 40-78 — "The Root Cause for almost all Evils!" (The Strange Things that People Say and Do to Get more Money!) Book 078. (This Book contains many Colored Photographs with Fascinating Explanations!)

[_] 40-79 — "Orgimmick Gardening at its Best!" (HOW to Grow Delicious Satisfying Foods without a 10-Million-Dollar Investment!) By The Worldwide People's Revolution!® Book 079. (This Book also contains many Colored Photographs with Wonderful Explanations!)

[_] 40-80 — "Guaranteed Solutions!" (HOW to Solve our Local and Global Problems in the Most Rational Manner Possible!) Book 080. (See the Description on Amazon: because they Offer a ONE-MILLION-DOLLAR REWARD to anyone who can Prove our Selected King's Solutions to be WRong or Unworkable! Can you Beat that? Do you have all such Guaranteed Solutions? Only our Selected King has those Solutions: beCause God Blest him with those Provable Solutions, which can be Proven in any Courtroom with Law and Order.)

[_] 40-81 — "Mexicans are more Intelligent than Americans!" (A Unique Challenge to all Americans and Mexicans!) By The Worldwide People's Revolution!® Book 081. {NOTE: The Remaining 275 Inspired Books by the Author of this Book may only be found in English, until we can get them Properly Translated into other Languages. Shame on you People who Killed him, who Broke his Heart with your Unbelief. May God have Mercy on your Poor Wretched Souls.} †‡

[_] 40-82 — "¡Los Mexicanos son más Inteligentes que los Estadounidenses!" (¡Un Desafío Único para todos los Estadounidenses y Mexicanos!) By The Worldwide People's Revolution!® Book 082. {NOTA: Aquí está el primer Libro en Español, que puede no ser Perfecto; pero, es Perfectamente lo Suficientemente Bueno para Iluminar las Mentes de quien lo Estudia.}

[_] 40-83 — "Was Billy Graham Greatly Deceived?" (Giving Honor to whom Honor is Due!) By The Worldwide People's Revolution!® Book 083. {NOTE: If you know a Grahamite, please Direct him or her to this Inspired Book, whereby he or she might be Converted to the Truths within it, and thus be Saved from Grahamite Perversions. Thank you.}

[_] 40-84 — "The New MAGNIFIED Version of the Book of DEUTERONOMY!" (The Understandable Version of Deuteronomy in Plain English!) Book 084. This is actually one of the Best Books within the entire Holy Bible, and also one of the Longest; but, do not allow that Fact to Deter you by any Means: beCause, "the Bigger Book is Normally a Better Book," which is True of a lot of Books, including all of the above Books: beCause it is the Nature of the Holy Spirit to get into Long-winded Sermons, you might say, which is WHY the Apostle Paul Preached until Midnight in the Book of Acts, until some Boy fell from a Window and Killed himself, whom the Apostle Paul Raised Up from the Dead and went on Preaching until the Dawn of the Day! {See: **"The New MAGNIFIED Version of the Book of ACTS"** for the Finest of Details, Book 063.}

[_] 40-85 — **"All of the Arguments are in Favor of our Selected King, who has Zero Challengers!"** (Before you Attend another Election Deception, you should Carefully Study this Inspired Book with an Honest Open Mind!) **By The Worldwide People's Revolution!®** Book 085.

[_] 40-90 — **"A New Jerusalem in the Great State of Flexible Texas!"** (HOW to make Good Use of the Mississippi River!) **By The Worldwide People's Revolution!** Book 090.

www.ingramcontent.com/pod-product-compliance
Lightning Source LLC
Chambersburg PA
CBHW062335220526
45469CB00008B/2729